MW01712189

Tennis for Everyone

Uncommon Solutions to Common Problems

Second Edition

Charles Cunningham

University of Illinois at Chicago

Lecturer, School of Kinesiology

Men's Varsity Tennis Coach

KENDALL/HUNT PUBLISHING COMPANY
4050 Westmark Drive Dubuque, Iowa 52002

ISBN 0-7872-4620-4

Printed in the United States of America
10 9 8 7 6 5 4 3 2 1

Gayle - You mean everything to me

Leigh - You continue to inspire me with your energy and curiosity about life. I love you

Donna - For all that you have done for Gayle and Leigh

Contents

Preface

For a number of years students of mine, past and present, have been asking when I would write a book detailing my teaching philosophy and methodology. Apparently my approach to teaching positively influenced a significant number of students and I was encouraged to provide a more detailed presentation of the ideas discussed in the classroom.

Tennis For Everyone: Uncommon Solutions to Common Problems, is my response to a need expressed by students who continue to search for answers to problems which not only affect their tennis game but also affect their personal growth.

My work as a teacher and coach, coupled with personal life experiences, has convinced me that too many students mistakenly assume that it is possible and permissible to deal with the challenges in a game such as tennis in one way, and deal with the challenges in life in another. Over two decades of teaching has shown me that this is not so. Examples abound (some of which will be cited later) which show the two to be inextricably linked. It is because I have not found a tennis book discussing the two under one cover, plus the fact that my students have enthusiastically requested it, that I have felt compelled to undertake this project.

As I have researched this book, a key element which has become thematic throughout the text stands out - *the process leading to personal fulfillment in the games we play and the lives we live emanate from the same source; our capacity to see and act in accordance with reality.*

Many sources have contributed to my knowledge of the growth process and the challenges you may face along the way. I am sharing concepts and principles written by numerous experts in fields related to the study of human behavior but rarely written about in a book on tennis fundamentals. I am also sharing my own experiences which are the result of my desire to better understand, from inside-out, the steps leading to personal fulfillment; what drives me to succeed and what stands in my way. But, undeniably, my most compelling source has been my students who have put these theories to the test each day on court.

Each part of the book serves a unique purpose. In part one, Self-Discovery, I identify innate qualities of human existence, and discuss a few of the principles which shape behavior and influence your learning environment. In part two, Self-Direction, I show you how to program for success by setting your sights on a specific target, finding a reason to reach it, and recognizing the obstacles which may stand in your way. And in part three, Self-Management, I discuss the learning process, and how your emotions and mental outlook affect self-efficacy. Here I conclude the book with a few comments about four attributes essential to high achievement and personal fulfillment.

Tennis For Everyone is a tool that will aid you in your quest to grow, personally and as a student of the game. Its efficacy comes not from passive reading but from actively integrating these principles into real, on-court situations. This integration must be viewed as the first in a series of steps toward increased awareness of your capacity to grow, and of your being an active participant in the process. If you read this book and use it, with the open-minded approach I found necessary for its creation, I am sure you will find as much enjoyment in using these ideas to achieve personal success and fulfillment, both on-court and off, as I have in writing about them.

Acknowledgments

A textbook of this magnitude would not be possible without drawing upon the experiences and writings of other authors. While it is not possible to list, individually, all of the people who have contributed ideas to this book, there are a few who I feel deserve special mention by name. The writings of Robert Anthony, Nathaniel Branden, Victor Frankl, Ayn Rand, and Zig Ziglar, have provided valuable insight into the qualities of life closely linked to high achievement and personal fulfillment.

Much of my research has been the result of my work with the hundreds of students I have taught at UIC. Each student, in his own way, has been instrumental in showing me how the game of tennis is just another tool we use to better understand the game of life.

Finally, one more resource which has been important to the creation of this book has been my work with the campers at Camp Greylock for Boys, a relationship which began in 1977. The countless hours of teaching Greylock campers each summer has heightened my awareness of my responsibility as a center of influence in the lives of my students, especially children. Thanks Bert, for giving me the opportunity to share my teaching philosophy with you, and your Greylock family.

How to Use This Book

At the end of the book you will find summary sheets for each chapter for your use. Your final grade will be based, in part, upon your reading and summarizing a specified number of chapters which will be announced during the first week of class. On this sheet you are to summarize, in your own words, your opinion of each chapter you have read. While not required for your grade, you may cite two or more personal anecdotes to illustrate any parallels you see between how you have approached learning the game of tennis this semester and how you live. Also, because my interest is with *your perspective*, not a restatement of mine, there are no wrong answers. Your perspective will, by degree, be different from mine and from each of your classmates. I am more concerned with this uniqueness rather than your simply telling me that my ideas are right or wrong.

At the bottom of each summary I have included space for you to list 1 or 2 action steps that you think will help you more consistently move in the direction of your stated goals (optional).

Please note that the tear-out summary sheets must be used in order for you to receive credit toward your grade. You may turn in your chapter summaries any time during the semester, up until the final week of instruction. Because papers have a way of being misplaced over time, however, I suggest that you turn in each summary as it is completed.

Introduction

Before introducing the principles of skill development espoused by my philosophy, I offer a few words to help you get the most out of this book.

Past experience has taught me that you are taking this class with the expectation that you will be hitting tennis balls and hearing ideas that will improve your backhand, your serve, and maybe your knowledge of the rules. Because of this, you may choose to delay exploring this book since you will note, by reading the table of contents, that I devote little text to tennis-specific theory or technique. This expectation is understandable. I must, however, impress upon you the importance of the relationship between the on-court activity and the performance problems addressed in the text. In your quest to learn the skills of tennis, two challenges await you: 1) performance - proper tennis technique and 2) process - learning theory. The on-court drills provide the opportunity for you to develop proper technique. The book outlines the principles involved in the growth process and helps you understand and manage the on-court challenges you will face day-to-day. Therefore I encourage you to read the text early in the semester in order to get the most out of your tennis experience.

I have designed this class to be a "no brainer." Each chapter will present ideas designed to help you improve your tennis skills, but this improvement will likely be secondary to the enjoyment you will experience by playing the game in a non-pressured environment, and to the health benefits you will enjoy by engaging in a fun physical activity. You will not fail this class because you can not hit three forehands or backhands over the net to your partner. Or because you do not know how to keep score in a tennis match.

This book is not a panacea; the possibility exists that you will face problems affecting your personal growth that, while identified in one or more chapters, may require further analysis beyond the limited scope of my work. This book has been written to be "user friendly." It is informative and reality-based, yet readable and practical for any student who desires to use this class as a means of experiencing self-improvement.

Also, your efficacy with each principle in this book is by degree. My concern is not whether or not you have self-awareness, but with the acceptance and expansion of your present awareness of your internal and external world; not whether or not you have a self-concept, but with the evolution of your self-concept and its effect on your personal growth; not whether or not you have self-direction, but the extent to which your present choices are making you the architect of your development.

Your evolution as a person naturally presupposes some relationship with these principles, either implicitly or explicitly experienced. I am concerned with helping you see yourself as you are with what you have, so that you can use this awareness and the knowledge it provides to get the most from your potential.

Knowing you will begin a critical evaluation of both the text and this class from the very first day, let me conclude the introduction by summarizing a few of the philosophical principles which shape my teaching philosophy.

Of all the things I have learned about life during my evolution as a person and as an teacher, nothing is more important to us as human beings than understanding the order of the universe and our role in it. We have each been given the gift of life, within the framework of a flawless, self-consistent, and non-contradictory universe. And with this gift we are challenged to seek self-understanding at the highest attainable level. To achieve this end, we have been entrusted with the capacity to self-actualize, a quality of life distinguishing humans from all other living beings. By design, we have not been pre-programmed, and because of volition, we must each personally decide which of our actions are for life or against it.

What this means for you is that any course of action you choose, in a material or external context, becomes a measurement of how your self-understanding conforms with the laws which govern reality. When you act in a manner which contributes positively to the sustenance of life, you are authentic to reality. When you act in any other way, you are in conflict with reality.

Whether your stated purpose is to pursue knowledge or a grade, when viewed in the context of self-understanding it becomes clear that any skill learned or grade earned represents a means to an even greater end; how your experiences in this class improve your ability to understand your relationship to reality, which, for each of you, is the only path to self-actualization.

Also, the importance of self-esteem to human performance can not be overstated. One needs only to look at the number of books written on this subject and further, to the number of people who buy them. The bittersweet irony of our evolution as a species is that on the one hand, we control the direction of our lives and can shape our environment accordingly, yet, on the other, we are forced to nurture our self-concept with the only means of regulation being our interaction with reality. In other words, we have the capacity to lead fulfilling lives and at the same time we must constantly work towards this fulfillment in order to have a positive self-concept.

As your tennis instructor this semester I have an agenda for this class which, for some of you, may not be fully understood or appreciated until the semester nears its end. I am not here to teach you how to play tennis. Only you can teach you. Let me also state that this book was not written to transform your life. Only you can change your view of reality. First and foremost I am concerned with you as a human entity, and with the manner in which you choose to integrate this class into your personal agenda. You already have individuals in your life who, in one way or another, attempt to shape your destiny, whether you want them to or not. And I feel it is not my place in life to shape anyone's destiny but my own. My appreciation of the game is surpassed only by my appreciation of you, and my belief that your right to experience the game according to your own internal standard is inviolable.

Tennis for Everyone has been written to add clarity to your view of yourself and the game of tennis. And as you use the book and on court-experience to seek greater autonomy and self-understanding, you will find that the grade and learned skill, are just the beginning.

PART ONE: SELF-DISCOVERY

Chapter 1
The Mind

Of all the resources available to help you learn more about the game of tennis, none will be more important to your success in this endeavor than your "*Mind*," and the method of thinking you will exhibit this semester. So important is this faculty to your ability to improve your tennis skills, I have devoted the entire first chapter to explaining how the laws and principles which shape and influence the thinking process affect what and how much you will learn in this class.

To understand the need for a discussion of the mind, I offer three stories of former students. The first student, Joe, appeared to be typical of most students who enrolled in my class. My initial observation of Joe gave every indication that he was a good student possessing relatively sound academic skills, taking my class to improve his tennis skills.

It was only four weeks into the semester that I noticed Joe's attendance waning to the point where the chance of earning an "A" was becoming more jeopardized by each missed class (I should note that Joe lived in the student residence hall across the street from the tennis courts, a fact which made his irregular attendance even more puzzling). Thinking a mid-semester discussion was in order, I talked to Joe about his irregular attendance and the negative impact it would have on his grade. I also made a few recommendations for improvement. Despite my intervention and suggestions for getting back on track, Joe's attendance continued its downward spiral to the point where he failed the class.

Sam was another student in my class who like Joe, appeared to have good academic skills with a keen interest in learning more about the game of tennis. Sam, in fact, had played on his high school tennis team and was one of the more advanced students in the class, a fact which led me to believe that he, more than most other students, would more fully appreciate the opportunity to improve his tennis skills that my class would provide.

Attendance was not a problem for Sam early in the semester. He enjoyed coming to class and participating in drills. Unfortunately, however, his early enthusiasm and commitment to improving soon gave way to other priorities, which put Sam in a quandary. Based upon points earned by the final week of class, his only options were to accept a "B" for his final grade or take an "Incomplete" and earn the points for an "A" the following semester. While he ultimately accepted an "Incomplete," neither option pleased Sam; he needed an "A" to maintain his grade point average and, because he was on academic probation, he needed a passing grade in all of his classes. While I sympathized with his predicament, I could not give him an unearned "A." Sam's choices at this point, however limited, were simply a consequence of choices he had made during the semester.

(I should go on to say that Sam returned the following semester with the intent of completing the attendance requirements to change his grade from an "Incomplete" to an "A." Apparently, however, Sam learned little from his mistakes the previous semester, because he failed to find his way to class the few times necessary to remove the "Incomplete." He received an "E.")

Dawn's status as a student in good standing in my class became precarious from the second week of school. Her attendance was so irregular that after five weeks I assumed she had dropped the course. When I reminded students to check their point totals at the end of week six, Dawn was alarmed to find herself failing. Her reaction surprised me, since Dawn, like all of my students, could have confirmed her point status any time during the semester.

During a discussion about her status and options, Dawn decided she would attend my four other classes each day for the remaining two weeks of the semester. As it turned out, Dawn's only class before noon was mine, and by attending each of my classes during the final two weeks she earned the required points for an "A."

The three stories you have just read were chosen because each identifies the kind of problems I will be addressing throughout the text. What they also do is help provide a basis for a detailed discussion of the mind and the relationship between its function as a tool of cognition and the level of success you wish to experience.

With your immediate need being that of hitting a better backhand, I can understand why you might question the need for a lengthy discussion of an aspect of our existence thought to be implicitly understood; this is, after all, a tennis class, not psychology. The need for this discussion, however, comes from more than the problems identified in the three stories.

This need is fueled by the fact that I have an inordinate number of students who either fail to earn enough points for an "A," or they earn the "A" and learn little about the game of tennis in the process. The fact that a student in my class may fail to earn an "A" or experience improvement might not seem too unusual, after all, students fail to realize academic goals in other classes for any number of reasons. The difference, however, is the unique structure of my class, which allows a student to earn an "A" with minimal intellectual aptitude (with two grading options, students can earn an "A" without learning or improving their tennis skills). A student must devote a considerable amount of time and effort to learn the skills of tennis, the same as in any other class. Being sensitive to the academic challenges facing the average college student, however, I put as much effort into serving the needs of a student whose ambition begins and ends with earning a passing grade as I do into serving the needs of a student who genuinely seeks to hit a better backhand.

The need for a discussion of the mind in this text also becomes obvious when I consider the fact that students have struggled with my class even when they have been given information that would facilitate improvement, and at the same time, been given the intellectual freedom to accept or reject this information at their discretion. I allow each student the freedom to choose what and how he wishes to learn without the concern that this decision will negatively affect his grade.

How does one explain this phenomenon? How is it that a class designed to help students learn and have fun in a non-threatening environment can become, for some, a forum for failure? What makes it possible for a student to fail a class in which he can earn an "A" while demonstrating little cognitive effort?

From the day I began researching this book, I knew that traditional methodology would not answer these questions because their origins do not depict traditional problems. They are unique in that they represent some of the problems you must face when you have to set the agenda, when you have a number of options from which to choose, and when motivation is primarily intrinsic.

Any attempt for me to help you succeed this semester without first addressing the function of the mind as the locus of mental and physical activity, would be an attempt to treat the symptoms adversely affecting your performance rather than the cause. If the problem is an errant forehand or poor attendance, then the cause is *cognitive inefficacy* or *failure to think*. Any problems you experience in pursuit of your goals this semester will begin and end with the breadth and depth of your thinking each day in class. And the manner in which you use the principles discussed in this, and other chapters, will ultimately determine your degree of efficacy. You must ask yourself, *will my mind produce success or failure*? While this correlation between the mind and performance may seem to be stating the obvious, my motivation for devoting a chapter to this relationship stems from the problems experienced by a number of former students, leading me to believe that some students come to me with the mistaken notion that the only tool they will need to succeed in my class is a tennis racquet.

The three stories introduced at the beginning of this chapter depict three ways in which students fail to achieve success in my class. And while one scenario may unfold in a manner slightly different from another, each is inextricably linked to the principles I will be discussing here, and in subsequent chapters. The journey toward self-understanding, and applying these principles to your performance in my class begins with the acceptance that there is no viable substitute for the mind as your primary tool for success. And it is only after this acceptance that the process of achieving success and personal fulfillment can begin.

Since it is known that your being here presupposes a working knowledge of the mind as a tool of cognition, I will begin by discussing the reason students often take my class and assume they will not have to think to achieve success. It starts with the concept of *values*.

Values estimate the worth you attach to certain aspects of reality which you consider important to your survival. Values are experienced by contrast - *I view this as important to my life as opposed to that.* This says that you can not value an aspect of reality on one level without comparison to an aspect of reality on a lesser level. (you should note that any aspect of reality not in your range of awareness - via volition or otherwise, or which you do not consider essential to your survival, is considered to be a non-value.) Values may be categorized into two classes: *concrete* and *floating*. Concrete values are those you consider inviolable, meaning they are your highest values and are never sacrificed to lesser or non-values. Floating values are those whose worth is measured more by circumstance than by concrete ideals.

Values are a necessary part of your evolution and serve as your means of distinguishing those aspects of reality essential to your growth and development from those which are not. That you value one aspect of reality over another is not as important as what aspect of reality you choose to value.

Before continuing my discussion on the importance of values, I need to discuss one important function of the mind that makes the possession of a value system essential. The ability to think is one of man's most distinguishing attributes, placing us above all other living entities in the context of being able to adjust our environment to our needs and our thinking to our environment. Further distinguishing us from other living entities is our ability to choose how we deal with reality. It is our ability to choose which makes the possession of a rational faculty so important because, by design, we are able to choose the manner in which we live, and, therefore, must shape our environment accordingly.

The ability to choose, however, does not come without a price. While we do possess a rational faculty which enables us to deal with reality on a conscious level, *we do not do so automatically.* While we have the ability to choose to contribute to the preservation of life - not destroy it, *this choice is not automatic.* While we have the capacity to adjust our environment to suit our needs, *this adjustment is not automatic.* Each is an act of *volition.* Volition means we have freedom of choice. The freedom of choice in what we think, what we feel, how we live, and how we perceive reality. But having the freedom to choose does not guarantee that how we choose to act will be productive. The privilege of volition gives equal time to actions which may destroy life or sustain it.

Let me elaborate further on the concept of values. The importance of a value system to us as humans has been underscored by the behavior of every student who has taken my class. As part of my research into actualizing human potential, I sought to discover how a student would behave when put in an environment where the potential for failure would be minimized - intellectual aptitude would be downplayed and he would be made to understand that the faculty of reason would be his primary tool of survival during our eight weeks together.

I found that students who achieved worthy goals in my class, the grade of "A" or improved tennis skill for example, have done so because of concrete values. These are the students who have taken my class and rarely missed a day. Often, when I would talk to a student embracing such dedication, his only response would be that he behaves in this manner because it makes sense to him. I interpret this as saying that he does it because he holds the values of responsibleness, commitment, and actualizing his potential as concretes. It is no surprise to me when I later discover that this student exhibits similar behavior in other classes more closely linked to his career goals.

This behavior is in stark contrast to that of the student who fails my class or experiences little skill improvement. This student often holds values similar to those of his peers who have succeeded. The difference, however, is that unlike his peers, his values are not concrete. They are floating. A student often behaves in this manner when he perceives my class has limited academic value and believes it is permissible to leave reasoned-judgement on the doorstep of the tennis courts, and pick it up when he departs.

The existence and possession of a system of values to guide our choices and actions is just the beginning. As part of our evolution we inherit a system of laws which, through the process of integration, help us to responsibly manage our rational faculty and its powers of reason, cognition, and volition.

The first law I will discuss is the *law of cause and effect*. In its most fundamental sense, this law states that everything happens for a reason and that all action is precipitated by a causal agent. To deny the existence of causality means to accept, in some form, the doctrine of *determinism*, which suggests that there are effects in our world possessing no causal relationship other than to their own existence. To a man of reason, any suggestion that an action may take place without any causal relationship outside itself would be, in reality, an impossibility.

There are no accidents in nature, thus, there are no accidents in our existence. To return to the example of Joe, one of my students who managed to successfully achieve a failing grade, I consider this as extreme a case of blindness to the law of causality in an academic context as one could exhibit. Joe's behavior suggested a blatant disregard for reality, seeing no connection between his noticeable absence from my class and the progressive lowering of his grade. Even when we discussed his performance, it was apparent that Joe had no clue as to why he was failing my class, and subsequently, showed no evidence to suggest that he was the least bit interested in finding the answer.

In a broader academic context, I want you to think about the statement occasionally professed by a student that, *my professor did not give me the grade I deserved*. Maybe you have, at some time, been guilty of this distorted view of reality. The law of causality should tell you that any grade you receive is a reflection of the instructor's evaluation of your effort, albeit one which is often subjective. While you may occasionally be victimized by a professor who - to the benefit of his own irrational self-interest - deliberately lowers your grade (possibly denying or evading the evidence of his rational faculty), I find this to be the exception rather than the rule. The law of causality says, in effect, *that if you want to keep getting what you get, just keep doing what you are doing*. And this statement holds true whether your behavior is appropriate to your goals or not. By understanding the causal relationship between the choices you make in this class and the results they manifest, you know you can change the results by making different choices.

The second law is the *law of homeostasis*. Also referred to as the *law of equilibrium*, this law states that given a choice between what is familiar and comfortable and what is unfamiliar and uncomfortable, human tendency will be to gravitate toward the former. As different aspects of reality are experienced, you become familiar with those that are frequently repeated, and thus, you make choices accordingly. One important function of this state of equilibrium is that it helps create a filing system for the vast number of values you develop in the course of your life, some common to all areas of your existence and some more or less unique. And this state of balance, like your value system, must be experienced by contrast - any action, thought, or feeling bringing about this state, is chosen by virtue of its preference over some alternative.

Before proceeding to the next law it is critical that I draw attention to the relationship between the law of equilibrium and your value system, in the context of this class. The cyclical relationship between equilibrium and values will prove to be helpful to you or problematic, depending upon the method of thinking you exhibit this semester. Each day you attend class, you will be forced to confront and deal with two equally powerful aspects of your existence which only you can control: *your power of volition and your need for equilibrium*. If, for example, self-responsibility and actualization are held as concrete values, attending class with regularity will not only serve as validation of these values as concretes, but will also show that your power of volition is consistent or in harmony with your desire for equilibrium. With the obvious exceptions of personal emergencies, which are often unexpected and out of your control, attending class will never be viewed as a laborious encounter. In fact, attending my class will take on a sense of urgency consistent with other classes you may be taking, regardless of the number of academic credits it may be worth or its relative importance to your major.

If, on the other hand, you harbor floating values - reserving self-responsibility and actualization for classes deemed more important (your major, for example), with each class day you will be forced to consciously decide, *should I attend class today or sleep a little later? Should I attend today's lecture or go to the cafeteria since it is raining and I know we will not be playing? Should I skip class today since I left my racquet at home, even though I can still get credit for observing?*

For those of you concerned primarily with your grade, this understanding of how values influence behavior is of paramount importance, because, no matter how you prioritize learning, one aspect of reality stands above all others: you can not pass this class unless you attend.

Next is the *law of belief.* This law states that what you believe, with feeling, becomes your reality. The problem here is that this law holds true whether or not what you believe is true to reality.

In two decades of teaching I have yet to encounter a student who was able to consistently perform a skill (hitting a correct backhand stroke for example) in a manner inconsistent with the conviction of his own mind, regardless of any evidence of what is really true about his ability at the time. An example of this may be found in the science of "hypnotism," which is nothing more than belief combined with a little suggestion.

If I were to ask you to place your tennis racquet on the court and lift it above your head with one hand, you would have little difficulty honoring my request. The truth is, you have the physical strength to do so, and you know it.

If, on the other hand, you were given the hypnotic suggestion that your racquet was imbedded in the court and could not be lifted, and I made the same request, no matter how hard you tried, you would not be able to pick it up. It is not that you suddenly lost your strength. It is just that you believe you have. In both cases - picking up the racquet, not picking up the racquet - your belief system was at work. And the latter proves an important truth you must understand about the power of suggestion - *your imagination will always override physical strength, will power or determination.*

The power of self-suggestion is demonstrated frequently in class when students ask for help with a particular stroke. Often when a student asks for help with his forehand, and I ask him what he thinks the problem is, his initial response is, "I can not get enough power in my swing." As soon as he says he "can not," I know my effectiveness is minimized because even though I have the information he needs, and he has the ability to use it, the belief that he can not hit with more power becomes his "mistaken reality."

If you expect to experience any improvement in my class, one of the most important obstacles you may need to overcome is the power of your own belief system, a point so important that I must restate that, *what you believe, with feeling, becomes your reality.*

Next is the *law of control.* In the context of this class, this law states that how effectively you will manage your learning environment will be commensurate with the degree to which you feel you are in control of your life. Having an "internal" locus of control means you feel in control of your destiny in this class, whereas having one which is "external" means you do not. The degree to which you develop and exhibit this internal locus is the degree to which you accept the principle of self-responsibility.

Self-Responsibility means that if you fail to attend class, you are responsible for the consequences. If your backhand does not improve - because you fail to ask for or heed my advice - you are responsible for this effect. If you do not get the grade you desire - because of irregular attendance or participation - again, you are responsible for this effect. I relate this to the attempt of any student to absolve himself of the consequences of his actions with respect to the grade he may receive in a class with the statement, *my instructor failed me.* The grade you receive from your instructor represents his appraisal of the degree to which you fulfill the requirements of his class.

The final law is the *law of expectation.* This law suggests that your chances of passing my class and experiencing any skill improvement will be realized in direct proportion to your expectations. Having a positive expectancy set puts into motion actions which will move you in the direction of your goal. You will be more aware of and sensitive to your attendance and participation. Also, if one of your goals is skill improvement you will be more receptive to information related to stroke mechanics.

Expectations, of course, must emanate from a specific source. And that source is anticipated outcome. Numerous studies have been conducted of highly successful people in many diverse fields of endeavor. And the most striking and consistent characteristic shared by these successful people has been their ability to anticipate the positive outcome of an event well before the event takes place. It is because of this that I say that my expectations of you this semester will not be nearly as important to your success as the outcome you anticipate before you walk on the court.

Well now you have it. You started reading this book as the most advanced species in the universe, yet you had no instructions as to how to use your innate qualities, and no program to guide you toward your goals. Now you have some tools and instructions, and all that is left is for you to set your program. The end for you is greater self-understanding which will lead to high achievement and personal fulfillment. The means you have chosen is my class and the game of tennis. The ideas which follow, combined with the opportunity for practical on-court application, will bring you closer to this reality.

Chapter 2

Self-Awareness

As part of your progression toward greater self-understanding, "*Self-awareness*" is both a pre-condition and a consequence. You can not grow without gaining more knowledge about yourself and your environment, and it is your desire to know more which makes heightened self-awareness possible. Having discussed your evolution from the basis of the laws which govern behavior, we must now begin the process of looking at who you are, how you view yourself and your surrounding environment, and how this relates to your success in this class.

I will begin this chapter by describing an exercise you will participate in during the first week of class. It is an exercise I have used as an introduction to each college tennis course I have taught since 1982. It was used by my teacher when I took tennis as a college student, and, because of what I learned from this experience about awareness and personal growth, I knew it would always be used as an introduction to any class I would be asked to teach.

The exercise begins with you standing in a line shoulder to shoulder with other classmates. Alternating from one end of the line to the other, each of you must walk ten steps forward, turn around, and upon returning to your place, you are to say your name aloud for the other students to hear. This pattern continues until each student has completed the exercise.

What I ask at this time is, how did you feel during the exercise? What did you observe about your behavior and the behavior of other students in the class? Was your attention drawn more toward what you felt, or what you perceived? Were you indifferent about what you experienced, or was there any particular emotion you felt toward your actions or any of the participants? What did you see as its relevance to your desire to learn more about the game of tennis?

How does this relate to self-awareness? Self-Awareness is *knowledge*. It is knowledge of your perception and integration of every aspect of reality. It is the sum total of what you feel, think, aspire to, love, and hate. It is your motivation, what you feel toward others, your habits, and your moods. Self-Awareness represents the range of knowledge of your internal and external worlds, the depth of this knowledge, and the level of desire you express to know reality and expand this knowledge. It is also qualitative with respect to what you feel toward your ability to know, in particular, yourself.

Let us return to the exercise I have just described. I use this exercise to get an idea of the extent to which students perceive, acknowledge, and evaluate the total tennis environment. Some students will laugh during the exercise; a few may appear to be a little anxious when standing out alone; one student may go out of his way to remove any doubt about his shyness; still another, by his body language and facial expression, may make it clear that the exercise is uncomfortable.

On this level, an explicit statement is made by each student about what he perceives, acknowledges, and thus, evaluates. On another level, I discover a little more about my students and their present awareness by asking the following: what was the most significant difference expressed by each of you during the exercise, and what, if any, was the most significant similarity? Other than observing that each classmate walked ten steps and returned while saying his name, students have offered little more in the way of an answer to either question. How about the fact that you each have a gait or stride pattern uniquely your own? Or that some of you walk faster than others? Or swing your arms differently? On another level, what about the thoughts and feelings represented by your walking style? How about the fact that, given these differences, you each accomplished the task by placing one foot on the ground in front of the other? Or that no one displayed an ability to defy gravity. Or the fact that because of your rational faculty and its power of volition, you each decided independently whether your thoughts should be directed inward or outward?

What may sound a little esoteric does in fact have significant relevance to your skill improvement. The game of tennis, just as life, is self-consistent and non-contradictory and requires that you work within the laws of physics and reality in order to experience success. Understanding the game, therefore, presupposes a degree of self-knowledge, and the range and depth of this knowledge is controlled by your awareness.

My point is that it is common for a student to approach my class with some trepidation, brought on by a comparison between his present skill level and the skill level of another classmate. First, you should know that your grade is in no way based upon how you perform in relation to how your classmates perform. Second, your grade will be performance-based only if you choose this grading option. Third, you should know that many students take my class who already possess tennis skills beyond the beginner level. Students enroll in my class for different reasons. And even if their reasons are unrelated to learning more about the game, or if they already possess skills beyond the scope of the class, this should not affect how you feel about the skills you presently own.

I use this exercise to allay some of the initial fears you and other students may harbor. I want you to know that if just finding the tennis courts or figuring out how to get the racquet out of the cover is a great challenge, then, rest assured, you are in the right place.

As for the differences pointed out by this exercise, I can understand if you were to question their relevance to the purpose of learning more about the game of tennis. I use them to draw attention to the fact that your success with the game and this class rests, in large part, with your first learning to accept who you are, what you have, and where your game is in the present moment.

To further this process of heightening self-awareness, I would like you to ponder a few more questions which arise from this exercise. How comfortable were you when it was your turn to proceed across the court? How did you feel both during your walk and just after you finished? On a different level, were your thoughts focused more on yourself during the exercise or on your classmates? Was there any noticeable change in the level of anxiety you may have experienced from the time you were waiting your turn, to just prior to walking, to actually walking, and finally returning to your place in line?

Your responses will significantly impact how you respond to the challenges you will face in this class. Learning or improving a skill necessitates a good deal of focused attention, therefore, it is important that you know what is essential in terms of the direction of your thoughts, and the feelings they create.

A necessary condition for improving your self-awareness is having the *desire* to do so. For you to change anything about your existence - that which is within your volitional control - there must be present some desire to make the change. With self-awareness, this means that you have made a conscious decision to expand what you know about yourself in the context of your cognition and integration of reality, and what you may feel or experience at any given moment or on any given level. Each day you attend class, you must answer the question, *do I stay within the comfort of my present level of awareness or do I risk giving attention to a new and unfamiliar aspect of reality for which I have no guarantees, but which may prove to be the key to attaining my goals*?

This class, like any class you may be taking this semester, will introduce information designed to assist you in your effort to realize established goals. Much of this information will be more or less familiar to you based upon your existing knowledge of the game of tennis and the process of personal development. As long as the information I provide is within the established limits of your awareness, little effort will be needed for you to acknowledge and integrate this information from day-to-day.

Obviously, however, most of you are here because you want to learn something new about the game of tennis, and this means you must, at some point, express a willingness to acknowledge and integrate information beyond that which you already know. It is in this endeavor that most students find the greatest challenge.

You will come to class each day looking to satisfy needs and fulfill expectations that are consistent with your value system. You may recall my discussion in the previous chapter about how your value system is like a clearinghouse in which you evaluate and categorize each aspect of reality you perceive. What this also means is that when you are confronted with new information, through a process of selective perception, you quickly determine whether this information is pertinent to your goals or not.

My class structure, and the fact that your grade is not affected by what you accept or reject intellectually, makes the challenge of integrating new information a bit more difficult. It is obvious that I am providing information which reaches well beyond the boundaries of learning how to hit a topspin serve or how to score a tennis match. It is, therefore, quite obvious that much of what I write about and will be discussing in lectures will challenge you philosophically and psychologically. If there were a connection between this information and the grade you desire, it would be in your best interest to integrate as much of this information as you deemed necessary to receive your desired grade. However, because there is no direct connection between the two, if this information is inconsistent with what you currently believe, this process of integration will become extremely laborious, since there are no tangible benefits to be gained by doing so, only the discomfort of deviating from the known and the familiar.

It is essential that I stress the importance of your dealing with the issue of self-awareness and desire as early in the semester as possible, for, as the experiences of former students has shown, the entrenchment of existing and long standing beliefs void of any tangible reward, make it likely that any expression of desire will become more remote as the semester draws to a close.

I should add that this issue is a non-factor for any student taking my class for reasons other than learning a new skill or improving an existing one. It only serves to remind you that no matter how far apart we may be philosophically, you must be careful not to let this difference draw your attention from the two tasks upon which your survival depends: *attending class and hitting tennis balls.*

As you move toward increased self-awareness the need for optimism becomes more evident. Once you set worthwhile and realistic goals in my class, your outlook will be positive to the degree that you feel you are improving, the hard evidence being your success with hitting more balls over the net, or feeling more comfortable with your swing. The trouble with learning, however, is that often, this evidence is only experienced after days or weeks of performing a particular skill. This is especially true when learning a new skill. It is during these moments (when evidence of learning is absent) that the need for optimism is of paramount importance.

Optimism is like a life preserver. As you endure the time-consuming process of learning, it is your inner belief that you are moving in the right direction that fuels your desire. Experience has shown that there is a connection between your ability to believe that you will realize your goals and your ability to keep them in sight. Students have lost sight of their goals in this class for any number of reasons, and some of these reasons have had little or no direct connection to the class itself. Reasons such as progress being slower than expected, comparisons to other classmates, personal problems which affect attendance, or setting unrealistic goals have all in some way resulted in lowered expectations for some students.

While it is my hope that you will realize the goals you have set, reality tells me that you may, in your own way, experience moments of frustration during the process. The challenge for you is to not disown or resist any feelings of frustration you may experience but to be aware of these feelings and accept them as part of the learning process, for it is only after self-acceptance that you can proceed to change.

Because of the cyclical relationship between your performance in my class and your overall sense of self (your performance day-to-day will affect your sense of self and your sense of self will thus affect how you approach my class) I will briefly address the need for optimism in a broader context. The history of this class has shown that when students take my class for reasons other than learning new skills or improving existing ones, they become more susceptible to external influences that conflict with the two requirements essential to receiving a passing grade - attendance, and hitting tennis balls. I draw attention to this because, given my class structure, when a student does find it difficult to show up and participate with regularity, what tends to be lacking beyond a sense of optimism in terms of learning tennis skills is a sense of optimism toward life in general.

I recall one particular student name Sue whose behavior in my class epitomized a rather pessimistic outlook on life. I had numerous opportunities to talk with Sue about her tennis and about life, due to the fact that most of the time when she did attend class she did not participate. Sue had the uncanny ability to always find something negative to say about her life, whether it was school and her disdain for some of her teachers, the part-time job she hated, or her inconsistent tennis serve. Needless to say Sue found life in general too formidable a challenge to face in a positive way, and attending class and facing the challenge of hitting tennis balls merely served as further evidence that the game of life was one she could not win. For two semesters Sue was engaged in a vicious cycle. She would come to class with low expectations and a poor sense of self. This in turn made it difficult for her to experience improvement when hitting balls. This lack of on-court success reinforced her feelings of pessimism and these feelings often kept Sue from attending class, which was her way of protecting her ego. Consequently, it took Sue three semesters to do what should have only taken one.

While Sue's experience was more the exception and an extreme, I find it appropriate to offer this as an example of how your outlook in my class and in life can be critical to achieving your goals.

This leads to another dimension of self-awareness which is "self-responsibility." Each semester the number one question that demands an answer from me is who is responsible for the success of this class? My unequivocal answer is that each of us, teacher and student alike, is responsible for his individual success. *We are collectively responsible for the success of the class.*

Essential to your success is understanding that awareness is knowledge; that each person is responsible for his awareness and ultimately how this aids or hinders his personal growth. What this translates into for you is that I can not teach you anything without your consent, which also means you can not learn from or experience anything outside of your level of awareness.

It is not possible to grow from any experience or feeling without accepting it as part of your reality. This responsibility is a precondition for improving your tennis skills or receiving a satisfactory grade, or both. If, for example, you do not realize your performance goals or receive the grade you desire, self-responsibility dictates that you first look to yourself, your behavior and thought patterns as opposed to reaching for external solutions such as the class structure or teaching philosophy. If you are not showing up for class with regularity, you are responsible for failing to see the connection between your grade or any learning you may desire and your attendance. If you fail to learn new skills or improve existing ones even when you attend class everyday, you are responsible for failing to integrate the information provided to you that is relevant to these needs.

You will hear me repeatedly say that no matter where the ball goes when it leaves your racquet, you can not dispute the fact that you alone are responsible for where it lands. If it lands across the net or across the street, if it goes into the net or into the stands, the fact remains that you were the causal agent of which your shot was the effect. Your tennis racquet is merely a tool which responds upon command. The same holds true for your awareness and its relationship to what you will learn in my class. Not only are you responsible for where your arm directs the ball, but you are also responsible for your level of awareness and the direction of your thoughts and beliefs.

This means you must accept as your own, everything which becomes part of your awareness at any level, whether it is perceived as good or bad, relevant to your goals or not. Thus self-responsibility becomes a commitment to awareness, and in the context of my class, a commitment to awareness of what is essential to your success, be it an improved backhand or a passing grade.

Self-Responsibility and the commitment to awareness is just as important to your success in my class as in any other you are taking. The difference, however, is that the importance of these concepts to your success in my class may be obscured by the fact that no tangible reward is available for your acceptance of this principle as essential to goal attainment.

The responsibility of attending class would be no less a decision within your volitional control even if perfect attendance was required for an "A." If my class was structured in this manner you would probably be more inclined to consider the importance of attendance when deciding whether or not to attend, because external factors critical to your success have caught your attention on more than a superficial level. If I decided to base your final grade totally on performance objectives - how much your tennis skills improved over the course of the semester, again, this approach would more likely catch your attention on more than a superficial level because of external factors I control.

The principle of self-responsibility spells out the student-teacher relationship we must nurture during the semester. It is a partnership in which I am responsible for giving you the best information available that will help you learn more about the game of tennis and creating a learning environment that will allow you to realize your goals. Your side of the partnership is to acknowledge your role as the causal agent for whatever takes place, as the information I present can not be integrated without your consent, a critical process which starts and ends with your level of awareness.

Finally, if self-responsibility is an essential part of the process of self-awareness, then "self-acceptance" must be viewed as its precursor. Self-acceptance is a non-judgmental acknowledgment that every relationship with reality which you experience you own. It does not mean that everything in your life is perfect. It does mean that what *is, is*, and that occasional failure must be embraced along with success.

For a number of years, even as I was researching this book, my knowledge of this concept, and its relationship to my teaching, was limited. For a long time I held firmly to the belief that it was harmful to my student to acknowledge what was being felt or physically experienced, if his feelings or experiences were not consistent with those he was attempting to create.

An example of how I mistakenly attempted to shield a student from a necessary aspect of development was my work with Tom, a student who took my class several years ago, and later continued taking lessons from me privately. I recall how I would ask Tom how he felt about a particular stroke we were working on in a lesson. Whenever Tom would tell me how he felt about the stroke and what he was feeling, if it was negative or inconsistent with what we were striving for I would quickly point out that it served no useful purpose to talk about anything negative or incorrect that may have been occurring at the moment. I was only concerned with reaching the goal we set, oblivious to what Tom may have been genuinely experiencing at the moment. As I continued to insist that he disown what he was experiencing when it was undesirable, it was not long before feelings of guilt began to surface, and eventually, rather than tell me what he was really experiencing, Tom would tell me what he knew I wanted to hear, because his desire to feel accepted by me became more important than being honest.

Needlessly to say, Tom and I spent more time than was necessary on some of his strokes, primarily because I would not allow him to fully acknowledge and accept his feelings, whether they were appropriate to his goal or not.

My experience with Tom, and many other students like him, taught me that the first step to solving a problem is to face it, an attribute you too will find critical to learning the game of tennis. The process of learning and improving tennis strokes is laborious and, at times, frustrating. The more unfamiliar you are with the basic strokes and movement skills, the more discomfort you may face as you struggle through the process of learning. Any attempt to disown the feelings of discomfort which your actions create can only lead to guilt, despair, and ultimately, to lowered aspirations.

Because the number of students enrolled in my class allows limited individual attention, the concept of self-awareness assumes even greater importance since the student-teacher ratio will make it necessary that you act as your own coach most of the time. Just as I learned the importance of self-acceptance from my perspective as your instructor, I ask the same of you in terms of how you handle the trial and error process inherent in learning or improving your tennis skills.

I mention this because the potential for negative habits to linger and become more ingrained is more likely when I am not available to assist you. Over a period of time, the lack of noticeable improvement, coupled with the feelings you may or may not be aware of and certainly not be able to express, may frustrate you to the point of lowering or abandoning your goals just as Tom did in the above example.

How you deal with the concept of self-awareness, particularly in terms of integration, will greatly influence how you deal with the remainder of this book as well as your efficacy with learning the tennis skills that will be introduced. For those of you here only to receive a passing grade, your level of awareness and the principles it subsumes may end with this chapter. For those of you here to gain a greater understanding of the game and of yourself, this chapter is just one more step in the process.

Chapter 3
Self-Concept

The "*Self-concept*," which is the human attribute used to identify, measure, and evaluate your interaction with reality, is one of the most important tools you will have to work with in this class. Having a positive self-concept is essential for those of you who want to expand your knowledge of the game, and in this chapter I will discuss how it is formed, its three basic components, and how it will influence your performance, both on-court and off.

Self-Concept in its broadest context is the sum total of what you think and feel about every aspect of the way you relate to reality. Your composite self-concept contains an unlimited number of mini-self-concepts which, once identified, are continuously measured and evaluated. For example, you have a self-concept as a student, and on another level you have a different self-concept for your performance in math as opposed to biology as opposed to history as opposed to tennis. This is to say that you may have a generally high regard for your academic skills overall, yet feel less regard for how you perform in one or more specific subject areas.

The degree to which your overall self-concept is positive or negative is a matter of choice - what aspects of reality you choose to integrate and your estimate of this relationship. As a student in my class, for example, your self-concept is formed and can only be measured by performing.

With this basic understanding of the self-concept as the controlling mechanism for your performance, I will now address the three dimensions of the self-concept, the first being the "self-ideal." The self-ideal is the way you dream of performing or would like to perform, as opposed to the way you may be performing now. It is the way you envision your performance under the most ideal conditions. One label which could be used to describe your ideal is the desire to be a *success*. While each of you may have different career goals, I know each of you would eventually like to be considered successful in your chosen field. I feel it safe to say that each of you, for example, would like to improve your tennis skills. The question which comes to mind is, *by what means are you to know when you are successful*? Each of you may have a different way of defining success. But however defined, this benchmark for the self-ideal is formed in one of two ways: externally, by adopting someone else's standard; internally, by setting your own.

What follows is the method I have used to help my students become aware of and understand the self-concept. In our first on-court session, students hit balls with a partner while I walk around and observe their strokes. During this observation I offer no advice regarding stance, grips, or swing, even when some students, vehemently professing that they do not know how to hit the ball, request it. An important part of this observation is listening to each student's "self-talk," or what they say to themselves about their performance.

This exercise in self-disclosure unveils a number of performance characteristics beyond each student's physical skills. Each, in his own way, reveals more than just the extent to which his self-concept is positive or negative, but it also reveals the extent to which his self-ideal has an *internal* or *external* locus of control. During this exercise I randomly ask students to assess their performance. Often a student will respond with a negative statement such as, "I have a lousy forehand swing," to which I ask, *if you had no previous knowledge of a correct forehand, and as your teacher I told you that your forehand swing was correct, would you still consider it lousy*?

I ask this question to draw attention to the problem you will face when your present level of performance is measured and evaluated against an external self-ideal. Any indictment of your existing tennis skills in this manner is unwarranted, especially if you are playing the game for the first time. One reason for this is the fact that we live in an external world where we often judge our performance on the basis of what we see in others, and do so even in the absence of supportive evidence. This form of self-criticism comes easy to an individual whose sole means of self-validation emanates from external standards of behavior. There is a direct link between this phenomenon and having an overall poor self-concept, a point which will be clarified as we move further along in this chapter.

For now, however, I will say that modeling an external standard can be very helpful, especially if you are learning the game for the first time. But you must make sure that your aspirations do not lead to a negative assessment of your present level of performance. This word of caution stems from the self-talk I have listened to from tennis players at all levels. And it is no wonder that many players spend years playing the game, even taking lessons, yet invariably find themselves frozen at a particular level of performance, a pathology caused less by limited physical skills than by harboring distorted beliefs.

Further, this exercise draws attention to the self-ideal, and the importance of balancing the external ideal with one which is internalized. I illustrate this by giving my class two tasks to complete. The first involves hitting balls with a partner without concern as to the number of balls being hit. The second task involves hitting ten consecutive balls on one bounce. During the exercise I give no requirements as to where students must stand, how to hold the racquet, or how to swing at the ball. This exercise reveals two things about the self-ideal: what my students know about the game and what they know about their skill limitations. Consistently, I find the majority of my students beginning this exercise by attempting to hit the ball with their partner using the full court and the full length of the racquet. For many students, particularly those playing for the first time, these conditions make the task of rallying quite difficult.

I observe the activity of my class for a brief period before bringing the group together for an explanation of the self-concept and how the degree to which they successfully completed the exercise was influenced by the self-ideal. When I ask how many students successfully completed each task few hands are raised. Usually the student who is successful is the student who already possesses skills beyond the beginner level. For the lesser skilled student, failure to complete the exercise occurred because he allowed the external self-ideal to override his existing level of performance. Stated another way, *his ambition exceeded his present ability*, something I find to be true most of the time when a person experiences a performance error. I tell my class that it stands to reason that as a beginner, which by definition this class caters to, you currently do not possess the necessary skills to be able to hit the ball using the full court and racquet. Ideal intentions are virtuous, however, any attempt to do what you know to be correct conceptually, without the skills to match, will always succumb to reality.

To illustrate this point, I will take one student (usually one who has expressed difficulty with hitting the ball), and use him to demonstrate how easy it can be to hit ten consecutive balls over the net when you allow the internal self-ideal to govern your actions. By having him stand a few feet from the net, holding the racquet half-way up the handle, and hitting the ball soft enough to just clear the net, this student proves that even the most inexperienced student can complete this exercise. And all I have done is make the playing conditions more realistic to the student's existing ability.

This exercise demonstrates just how easy it is for a student learning the game of tennis to allow his behavior to be influenced by what he sees others doing without regard to his existing skills, however limited these skills may be. In fact, I would go so far as to say that in my teaching, I find this to be one of the primary and most challenging problems I must deal with in helping students progress beyond the basics of the game. What I tell students who experience this difficulty is that idealizing, unlike reality-based behavior, has no time element and requires no physical effort. So to hold any external ideal as anything more than a model becomes a sure set-up for failure, as many of my students have discovered.

One more point I wish to address regarding the self-ideal as a component of the self-concept, is how easy it is to form a negative or poor self-concept by holding what I call a *false ideal*. As you recall, I stated that your self-concept can only be formed by the identification and integration of some aspect of reality - you must first be aware of something you want to do and then you must attempt to do it. Without identification and integration, nothing exists by which you can form a self-concept, either positive or negative, which also means, in this context, you can not possibly have a self-ideal. Let me explain.

Occasionally a few students will come to me at the beginning of the semester and profess categorically that they have never played the game and would not know how to begin to hit even one ball over the net. The apprehension felt by these students is often heightened during the initial on-court session by the fact that I am asking them to demonstrate a skill they do not believe they have and to do so in front of classmates they do not even know. After observing these students go on court and demonstrate, quite successfully, the skills they claimed they did not have, I proceed to address the blatant contradiction between what they initially said and how they eventually performed.

First there is the implicit knowledge of the game these students possess - they have identified the game as an activity they wish to pursue - thus providing a reason for taking my class. This identification means they have, at some time, seen someone playing the game which implies that they have some awareness of where to stand, how to hold the racquet, how to swing at the ball, and where to hit it. Any direct observation of a desired skill implies at least a cursory knowledge of the skill. To understand this, I ask, *would you (as a student) take a class without having some knowledge of its relationship to your academic goals, or pursue a skill without some idea of its relationship to a currently held value*? What I know about self-awareness and your value system tells me that any student taking my class will at minimum be able to find the court, get his racquet out of the cover, and under the right conditions, be able to hit a few balls over the net.

Second, because these students have made a sweeping indictment of their tennis skills even before attempting to hit a ball, they are guilty of either harboring a false ideal or attempting to deny evidence provided by the senses. Awareness brought them to my class, a fact that implies at least a cursory knowledge of what the game entails. And because they have never hit a ball, I can only conclude that the false ideal these students hold is the result of a poor self-concept.

As you can see, the self-ideal as a component of the self-concept reveals a number of performance problems related to what you think and how you feel about your performance abilities. While the self-ideal reflects the performance model you wish to emulate, the next component of the self-concept, the "self-image," reflects what you see as the truth about how you perform.

The self-image is the imagined self, brought to life in words, pictures and experience. The difference between the self-ideal and the self-image is that the self-ideal reflects the standard of success you wish to achieve, while the self-image reflects what you ultimately believe to be true, based upon whatever evidence you decide to accept.

Your self-image is like a thermostat upon which your performance is a setting. What is good about this is the fact that whether it is high or low, *you control the setting*. Where you choose to set your performance, however, is influenced by your belief system, which is your assessment of your current performance ability. The self-image is your belief system brought to life, and just as a thermostat does not allow a room to get too hot or too cold, your regulated self-image does not allow your performance to move too far above or below where you believe it should be. Self-image is the causal agent of which your performance is an effect, thus, my purpose here is to help you create a positive self-image that will manifest itself in the performance you desire.

To begin this process I should state that I can not, through this book, give you a positive self-image. My ideas are designed to help you become more aware of the relationship between what and how you think about your performance day-to-day and what you actually experience. Your self-image is a statement about how you see you in action, and *if you want to change your performance you must first change the image you create*. What I hope my ideas will do is help you change the truth about what you see. Because, no matter what I discuss about developing a positive self-image, unless you already have one, what you believe and accept as the truth about your performance will always be filtered through and processed by your current level of awareness.

When introducing self-image awareness to my students, it is most important to me that the ideas I discuss have practical application - I want them to be able to apply these ideas to real on-court situations. As an example of the process I use to introduce this concept to my students, I recall a former student named John. John approached me one day in class saying he was having trouble with his forehand stroke and wanted some advice on how to improve. Whenever a student approaches me for help I always start with the question, *if it were your choice, how would you like to hit your forehand*? When I asked this question of John, his immediate reply was, "I can not hit the ball over the net!" Now the first problem with John's response was the negative over-tones, a self-indictment indicative of a poor self-image - at least regarding this particular stroke. Second, John did not correctly answer my question - *how would he like to hit his forehand*? Third, having seen John hit a few forehands over the net, I knew his assessment of his existing forehand was not exactly accurate.

I asked John the original question again, this time requesting that he tell me how he would like to hit his forehand and to show me his *ideal* forehand by swinging his racquet. This little question and answer session helped John see his forehand in a more positive way, and needless to say, as he improved the image of his forehand swing, the swing improved accordingly.

The approach I used with John is the same approach I use with any student whose performance problem is related to a conflict between what he wants to do and what, in reality, is actually occurring. The first step in the process is self-awareness in that you must understand that *what you get is what you see*. If you want to correct a problem with your forehand swing, you can only do so by accurately assessing the problem. Regardless of how you are hitting your forehand, the truth is, *it is your forehand*. This calls for self-acceptance. Second, the statement, "I can not hit the ball over the net," may not only be inaccurate, but it provides no information that will help correct the problem. If the ball is not going over the net, there is a reason for this. Remember the law of cause and effect. If you first identify the cause of the problem you can then begin to look for a solution. It is crucial, therefore, that you view your forehand with a non-judgmental eye. Finally, you need to create a mental image of the forehand you consider ideal by focusing on what you want to do rather than on what you can not do.

What you need to understand about the self-image is that it is one of the most powerful regulators of performance you possess. In fact, one of the most significant discoveries of modern day psychology has been the discovery that what you imagine gets stored in your system just as though you had actually experienced the event. What this means in terms of how you process information is simply this: *what you imagine becomes your reality.*

In working with students on self-image development I am learning more about the role this component of the self-concept plays in learning a skill, and more importantly, what you can do to make how you see yourself, and thus how you perform, more aligned with your self-ideal. When I say that the self-image is the imagined self, I mean this quite literally, much to the surprise of many students. To see how this works, close your eyes for a moment and, according to your standard of success, imagine yourself as having a backhand which mirrors your self-ideal. The first thing I want to know is, *can you picture your self-ideal and attach it to your backhand*? Second, *if you can do this, how does it feel*?

The significance of the first question is that many of my students experiencing performance problems find it difficult to make any connection between the ideal-self and the self they know, even in their head. What these students fail to realize is that the imagination allows each of us to be as successful as we choose to be. After all, who is going to know? And if you can not even pretend your backhand is successful, it is certain that you will not be able to experience it physically, because, *what you imagine becomes your reality*. This problem with the imagined self will be discussed further when I talk about self esteem.

The significance of the second question relates to the self-image as a regulator. Once you have established the setting, if your performance gets too far out of range, the image which you have created will bring it up or down depending upon whether you are performing above the setting or below. Occasionally a student will improve a stroke - let us say his backhand. Over a period of time, he will reset his performance of this stroke at a new level and become comfortable with this setting. If he occasionally performs below this new setting, the image tells him he is out of character, correction is made, and the image brings him back to where he belongs. What is also interesting is that this process works the same way when his performance exceeds the new setting. If he performs too well the self-image will invariably bring his performance back to the new lower setting.

Now you would think that with so much control over these two elements of the self-concept (your self-ideal which you create and your imagined-self which reflects the performance range you set) bringing the two together and experiencing the success you desire would, with the appropriate effort, be a reasonable expectation. Much has been written in the field of psychology about the self-concept, and one point universally agreed upon is the fact that "self-esteem," or what you think of yourself, is the most important element of the self-concept. Your self-esteem, which is the evaluative component of the self-concept, differs from the self-ideal and the self-image. The self-ideal may or may not be realistic and the self-image may be a mistaken truth about your performance capability. But what separates the self-esteem from the other two attributes is that, as an evaluative mechanism, *it is always true*.

Self-esteem is the estimate you place upon yourself in the face of reality. While no one condition, performance, or behavior is responsible for the self-esteem, every aspect of the way in which you relate to reality has an impact on the degree to which you feel *self-acceptance* or *self-rejection*. It is important for you to know that nothing in this class - my ideas nor the on-court activity - will give you self-esteem. What I hope you learn is that it is your responsibility to like yourself in spite of, and not because of, what you do with the game of tennis. This is to say that you can not get self-esteem from my class - *you must bring self-esteem to it.*

What makes this difficult is the fact that we live in a society in which a strong emphasis is placed on outcome or results. In tennis, for example, the bottom line is, *did you win*? *Is the ball in or out*? What becomes lost is the importance of "process" or the effort directed toward realizing a worthwhile goal. Self-validation runs deeper than any one deed, act, or accomplishment. As a student you must eventually come to accept a new reality which says that your value as a person is innate. You did not evolve into a worthy human being because of what you have done - *you were born that way*. And if your worth has not come from your accomplishments, it can not be taken away or diminished by your failures.

The importance of positive self-esteem to performance is too important to be overlooked in my class, regardless of your motives for being here. That is because experience has shown that everything you accomplish this semester - from improving racquet skills to learning the rules of tennis, to just earning a grade - will be achieved only through reasoned-judgement. And reasoned-judgement is your only means of knowing and accepting reality. And only a person of uncompromising self-acceptance is capable of fully accepting that what is, is.

For me to believe that I am capable of fulfilling the needs of every student in my class at every moment and not violate any needs you may have beyond the context of this class would not be realistic. It also stands to reason that your defining moments this semester will be the frequency with which you will be able to handle reality when reality is not what you want it to be. Should your goals go no further than receiving a passing grade, even this goal can become obscured, should you at any time feel less than competent to exist, a form of low self-esteem. Self-competency is an evaluative component of existence experienced only through your interaction with some aspect of reality. What makes self-esteem and the achievement of even the most elementary goals sometimes impossible is the fact that while the existence of reality is both self-consistent and an absolute, self-competency is not. *It requires effort.*

If positive self-esteem were an absolute and a given, and not something you must choose to develop, everyone would have it. The same would also be true of your existence to reality. If the choice to act to sustain life were a given and not an act of volition, then reasoned-judgement - in the context of life-sustaining action - would not be possible for you, nor would it be necessary. This process would be self-evident.

What you must face is the reality that positive self-esteem and productive action are both achieved through the effort of your mind. This, however, is not the problem you must resolve. The problem you must resolve is that of *having low self-esteem because you have decided that what you do determines who you are*.

The challenge of self-esteem takes on greater significance for those of you here to learn new tennis skills or improve existing ones. Each class will provide you with an opportunity to choose to act in a manner which is productive (relative to your goals) or destructive. The benchmark for your self-esteem in this context will be your ability to sustain and increase your self-acceptance, whether your actions are consistent with your goals or not.

The self-concept is a complex human attribute essential to goal achievement. As important as it is for you to have a goal, it is equally important that you understand the psychological process involved in its attainment. Developing a positive self-concept is just one step in this process, albeit an important one. And it is my hope that at some point you will discover that having a positive self-concept is both a pre-condition of greater self-understanding, and its consequence.

Chapter 4
Attitude

"Words can never adequately convey the incredible impact of our attitude toward life. The longer I live the more convinced I become that life is 10 percent what happens to us and 90 percent how we respond to it.

I believe the single most significant decision I can make on a day-to-day basis is my choice of attitude. It is more important than my past, my education, my bankroll, my successes or failures, fame or pain, what other people think of me or say about me, my circumstances, or my position. Attitude keeps me going or cripples my progress. It alone fuels my fire or assaults my hope. When my attitudes are right, there's no barrier too high, no valley too deep, no dream too extreme, no challenge too great for me."

The above quotation by Pastor Charles Swindoll was passed on to me in 1992, and so moved was I by its message that I found it necessary to make it the centerpiece of my lecture on attitude. This lecture is usually given at mid-semester after I have had an opportunity to evaluate the attitudes of my students based upon their participation and performance in class. And it is one of my favorite topics for discussion because of its importance to skill development, goal achievement, and personal growth. In this chapter I will discuss the importance of having the right attitude, how it is developed, and its impact on your success.

What is attitude? Attitude is a state of mind or disposition toward some aspect of reality, relative to its importance to your values or goals. You have an attitude about the weather, the clothes you wear, your performance as a student, your relationships with friends, your hobbies, your favorite foods, what is on television, and any number of things within your range of awareness. One thing you must understand, however, is that no matter what your attitude is toward any aspect of reality, your attitude is a description of how you interact with reality - *it is not who you really are*! When you decide that what you do is the truth about who you are, not only are you mistaken, but when you allow success or failure to define who you are, you are simply harboring a pseudo sense of self-worth, a point discussed in the previous chapter.

So before going into detail about the importance of having the right attitude I want to make sure that the distinction is clear between who you are on the one hand and what you do on the other. In the previous chapter we discussed the self-concept as the means through which you validate your existence, and the importance of expressing self-acceptance independent of your actions. The same must be said about attitude. In the context of my class, and learning more about the game of tennis, your self-worth must remain intact, regardless of any contradiction you may discover between the goals you set and the behavior you exhibit.

The importance of attitude to success has been demonstrated by the performance of my class. As part of my research, I reviewed the grades of former students dating back to 1985 and discovered that during this period approximately one out of every ten students earned a grade of "D" or "E." My search for answers as to why one in ten students would experience failure in a one credit-hour activity class where skill acquisition was not essential to success brought forth the importance of attitude and the difference between attitude and *aptitude*. While aptitude speaks to cognitive dexterity or skill, attitude speaks more to one's ability to recognize and act upon the essential tasks relevant to goal achievement. This is to say that the student who succeeds in my class recognizes the importance of attending class with regularity and does so; the student who fails does not. The student who succeeds in my class recognizes the importance of active participation and does so; the student who fails does not. In summary, whatever you do, whether it involves class attendance or participation in drills, your actions from the start are influenced by the attitudes you hold towards yourself and your proposed activity.

Having defined attitude, the next question is, *where do attitudes come from*? Attitudes toward life experiences come from our expectations about desired outcomes and the relative importance of these outcomes to our values or goals. No matter what ideas I present or how I present them, I know that your commitment to improving your tennis skills will be consistent with the degree to which you see value in improving and the degree to which you feel that improvement is possible.

Perhaps you are taking tennis because you are about to graduate and you need one more credit hour to fulfill your graduation requirements and only need a minimum passing grade of "C." On the first day of class you look at the syllabus and notice right away that to earn a passing grade, you only have to attend a certain number of classes and that you can earn a "C" without improving your tennis skills. If this is your goal, and you see that you do not have to improve your tennis skills to reach it, the idea of exhibiting behavior that will improve your tennis skills may never enter your range of awareness. You will find yourself attending class without trepidation or concern about failure or improvement because just the fact that you made it to class has already fulfilled the expectations you set. When you do attend class, you will make an effort to hit balls when and if you find a partner suitable to your needs, and if the practice conditions are to your liking. You will listen in class when ideas are presented to help you improve your tennis skills, but because learning will require expectations beyond those you have set, your attitude will cause you to dismiss anything beyond your expectancy set as being a non-value. Also, once you have earned your desired grade, you will no longer have a reason to attend class, except for any lingering desire you may have for exercise.

Maybe you are here because, besides the credit, you need an "A" to improve your academic status. On the first day of class you look at the syllabus and notice right away that to pass you have to attend a minimum number of classes, but in order to receive credit for attendance you have to participate - you must be on court hitting balls - but you do not have to learn anything or improve your tennis skills in the process. Once you see that your expectation of an "A" can be realized without any effort beyond just hitting balls, your awareness will immediately dismiss the possibility of exhibiting behavior inconsistent with your expectation. You will attend class regularly and you will make the effort to hit balls while in class, often doing so with a partner you do not like or even when the weather is not to your liking, all in the name of earning your desired grade. Occasionally you may even ask for help with a troublesome stroke or maybe with keeping score in a match. These moments, however, will be rare, and even when given advice, you will find it difficult to integrate this information because you have no vested interest in doing so.

The possibility exists that you may be here because you want to learn more about the game of tennis beyond what you have seen by watching other people play. The credit will count toward your degree and the grade is unimportant as long as you pass with at least a "C." On the first day of class you look at the syllabus and notice right away that the number of attendance points needed to earn a passing grade are minimal. When you signed up for the class you decided that your goal would be to learn how to consistently rally with a partner and improve your serve. With this expectation you will come to class each day with the desire to do more than just show up and aimlessly hit balls. You will come to class with an agenda geared toward self-improvement and occasionally ask for help in overcoming a problem with your technique. Even when forced to hit with a partner that does not exhibit similar effort, you will make your practice time count. Less than ideal weather will be embraced as a necessary obstacle to be dealt with in pursuit of your goal. You expect to improve and this will be reflected in your behavior.

Each of you will fit into one of these behavior profiles just described. Two profiles characterize a student concerned only with earning academic credit or a passing grade, and whose effort begins and ends within the limits of these expectations. The third characterizes a student who wants more than just the credit and passing grade. Here, the behavior depicts a student who also wants and expects to learn a new skill or improve an existing one, and is willing to put forth the effort necessary to realize this expectation. How would you describe your attitude when measured against each profile? Would you characterize the first two any different from the third? Further, should I look at you less favorably if you were to fit profile one or two rather than profile three? As a student depicting profile three, are you more likely to be successful in class than if you fit profile one or two?

Surprisingly, there is really no difference in the three profiles in terms of attitude. There is nothing about the behavior exhibited in profile three that would make it any more likely that you would achieve success over a student fitting the other profiles with respect to attitude. Your chance of being successful in each is the same. Why? Because each profile has one important thing in common - *each describes a student who has a goal or expectation to be realized, and they have the attitude to match the expectancy set.*

It is important to understand that your attitude will never be good or bad. It will always be either appropriate or inappropriate - *right or wrong* - for the expectations you may hold at any given time. If I say your attitude is bad because you are here for a reason other than learning, I am attempting to invalidate your view of reality by imposing my estimate of a good attitude on you. If you say your attitude is bad, You are showing a disregard for the principle of self-acceptance.

If you can not have a bad attitude, and if it can only be right or wrong, what can you do if you want to improve the attitude that you have? I have discovered that there are only two things you can do to improve your present attitude. The first is change your present behavior. The second is change your expectations.

If you are to change your present behavior you need to know what your behavior is, which means you need to know what qualities accurately define your attitude. A few years ago I was privileged to attend a seminar on attitude development conducted by Zig Ziglar, a well-known expert in the field of human potential development. As part of his presentation he asked the audience to create what he called the "dream employer/employee." This involved listing all of the qualities we considered essential to being an ideal employer or employee. The list we compiled included being organized, honest, flexible, committed, enthusiastic, dependable, cooperative, open-minded, creative, persistent, disciplined, a good worker, a good listener, self-confident, and self-motivated.

After identifying these qualities we were asked to categorize them as either skill - something that can be taught, or attitude - something experienced as a feeling, or a combination of both. In all, we listed thirty-eight such qualities of which seven were labeled a skill, thirty-one an attitude and all thirty-eight a combination of both. What I found interesting about the exercise was that, after some thought, every quality we considered important to successful performance *was both an attitude and a skill*, which suggests that any attribute linked to having a positive attitude is *teachable.*

Should you discover at some point during the semester that you need to change your attitude, all you need to do is look at the qualities you wish to emulate as a student of the game of tennis. What are these qualities? Some of the qualities essential to learning the game of tennis are patience, dedication, commitment, focused attention, having a disciplined work ethic, persistence, self-confidence, optimism, and courage. And because of the structure and philosophy of this class, you will also need to be self-motivated, self-responsible, self-reliant, and self-directed in order to improve your tennis skills. This may prompt you to ask, *which of these qualities, if any, do I already have*? The answer is that you, just like all students, have all of them, and a lot more. What you must understand is that you possess varying degrees of each quality. For you to decide that you lack confidence, discipline, responsibleness, or a sense commitment is not only a mistaken truth, but also a personal indictment which would only serve to damage your self-concept, or more specifically, your self-esteem.

For some of you, this is all that will be necessary for you to remain on target with your expectations in this class. If you are only here for the credit, you will have little need for patience, persistence, courage, or self-confidence. Your primary concern should be with your commitment to attending enough classes to earn the minimum passing grade. If you are only here to earn an "A," you will have little need for courage, focused attention, or optimism. Your primary concern should be with commitment and dedication. Only if you are here with the expectation of learning a new skill or improving an existing one will you need to be aware of the degree to which you exhibit all of the qualities mentioned above.

If you are here to learn, you must have the desire to do so. This takes us back to the concept of awareness. For now you must become aware of specific qualities you are exhibiting and you must be able to identify which of these qualities are inappropriate for your expectations so that the necessary adjustment can be made. For example. During the first two weeks of the semester you find it easy to improve your strokes. You are attending class regularly, you are working on specific goals with my assistance, and your expectations are clearly being realized. By week five, however, you notice that your progress has stagnated, you are not hitting with the consistency you expected after four weeks, and you begin to get a little discouraged and question whether your expectations are, in fact, realistic.

Assuming you have the desire to get back on track, there are a number of possibilities you could explore to identify the source of your problem. Maybe your attendance after the first two weeks became irregular because of personal problems or problems with other classes. If this is true then you only need to work on your commitment, dedication, and responsibleness. Having the right commitment, dedication, and responsibleness means that, while your life does not revolve around your tennis, you will do what is necessary to make sure that the interference of outside problems to your goal is minimal. If attendance is not the problem, what are you doing when you are in class? Is your attention as focused as it was during the first two weeks? Even when your attendance is regular and you feel you are working hard during drills, maybe you need to examine your work ethic. Your work ethic is actually three dimensional. Having a strong work ethic means you not only work with intensity, but you also work long enough to accomplish your goals and do drills specific to these goals. Maybe you are focused but not on the right thing. Maybe your attention is fine, but you are not putting forth enough effort. Maybe you are focused and intense but not working long enough when you are in class. How optimistic are you? Improvement is never experienced without occasional setbacks. If you spend too much time focusing on the brief plateaus necessary for improvement, you might easily become discouraged. And this could affect your commitment or dedication, and the amount of effort you display on court.

For many of you this process of behavior adjustment may be necessary at some point during the semester to ensure that your expectations are realized. What students in the past have discovered, however, is that it is difficult to adjust your attitude when you do not know your expectations. What do you expect from tennis? Were your expectations after week one the same as they were when you initially registered for the class? Are your current expectations the same as they were a week ago? Expectations may change at any time and for any number of reasons, however, what does not change is the fact that your expectations will always determine whether your attitude is right or wrong, not the reverse. This is to say that the "right attitude" can only be the attitude which most accurately reflects the expectations you hold at any given time.

How are expectations formed in this class? And can they be changed? The first thing I will say is that each of you had some expectation about tennis even before the first session. After all, how often do you take a class without some idea as to what you will gain by doing so? I know, for example, that you may have enrolled because you need the credit or an easy "A." Maybe you need a class where you can get some exercise, or, perhaps you are taking my class because you like what a friend has told you about my teaching style. It is possible that you already know how to play tennis and just want an opportunity to hit some balls. Still, you may know very little about how to play tennis, and have taken this class to learn more. The expectations that have brought you here may differ for each of you. This should not be your primary concern. Of greater concern is knowing whether or not you need to change your expectations. And if so, how do you do it?

From the very beginning of my teaching career I have had a sincere interest in student expectations, and why a student would chose the "path of least resistance" with respect to learning or improving his tennis skills. From the days when learning was a requisite for passing my class (through the use of written and on-court tests, for example), to where I now allow each student to decide, individually, what he wants to do with the game, one constant has been the fact that a significant number of students have chosen to limit their expectations to earning a grade or academic credit, or just the opportunity to hit a few tennis balls. Earlier in my teaching career I took a rather malevolent view of this phenomenon and considered these students to be lacking in motivation. Within the limits of my knowledge at the time, I did not know what else to think about students who would take a tennis class and show little desire to learn. As my teaching philosophy has matured, and as I have learned more about attitude development, I have found some answers which may prove beneficial to you, should you at any time find yourself unclear as to what your expectations should be, or how to change them.

We already know that expectations come from desired outcomes and the relative importance of these outcomes to your values. The question for you becomes, *what values should I use to determine the importance of my desired outcome in this class?* Having witnessed the performance of hundreds of students over the years, each with different goals and expectations, it has become clear that in terms of attitude development, this is one of the most important questions you can ask. And it is one only you can answer. Recalling my experiences as a college student, and listening to the stories of current and former students, I am not surprised that my class may be one of the few college classes which requires that you ask this question, and allows you to answer it with impunity.

How often are you given the choice of deciding for yourself, without undesirable consequences, the importance of course content relative to your current values? Traditional teaching carries the assumption that your expectations, and thus desired outcome, are both predetermined and consistent with the subject matter and the expectations of the instructor. And the evidence I have witnessed in support of this teaching doctrine is overwhelming. The one dimension of my class, which may set it apart from others you may be taking is that it allows each of you to decide where this class fits into the hierarchical structure of your value system. And for good reason.

To begin, you must understand that as your instructor I do not establish your values. You do. Only you can determine which aspects of reality are important to your existence and which ones are not. Further, you are responsible for the hierarchical structure of your values - what you value most at any moment and what you value least. The degree to which you manage this responsibility will significantly affect the extent to which your goals are realized. Because of past conditioning, most students take my class armed with the mistaken assumption that the tennis skills I present must be valued by all, at the same moment, and to the same degree. It is difficult to harbor any other expectations when most of the classes you may be taking divest you of this responsibility. What else can be said of a grading policy whereby each student must learn the same material to the same degree and within the same time frame? A student conditioned in this manner is destined to become lost in my class, because he may find himself at the end of the semester still waiting to be told what and how much he must learn about the game of tennis, and how soon he must learn it.

This phenomenon is evident each semester when students are given an opportunity to express their opinion of my class in an exit evaluation. When I first began this practice, the two primary complaints were: 1) "You did not teach me anything," and 2) "You did not make me learn." (Interestingly, since I introduced this book and students actually began reading it during the semester, these complaints have become less common.)

My vision for this class begins and ends with using the game of tennis to help you achieve greater self-awareness and self-understanding. Therefore my expectations can not be limited to how much you improve your forehand or backhand or what you learn about doubles strategy or how to keep score in a tennis match. I have chosen to leave expectations of this nature in your hands to reconcile individually as your needs of the moment dictate. The grading policy I have created serves as the litmus test which validates this purpose.

One could falsely assume that the only valid reason you could have for taking my class is to learn as much about the game of tennis as you can during the course of this semester. I contend that this reason is valid only to the extent that learning new tennis skills or improving existing skills is held at or near the top of your value structure. I ask, *how important is the subject matter in this class to your life right now*? As I researched this book it became increasingly clear that traditional teaching philosophy rarely affords a student the opportunity to answer this question. And because this opportunity is so rare, I have often found many students in the past either unwilling to answer the question, or incapable of doing so.

If you are to enjoy success in this class - defined as setting and achieving personal goals - this question must be answered. While I can not answer it for you, I know that, in terms of attitude, your expectations will be heightened to the degree that your perceived outcome is consistent with your current dominant values. Before you decide that skill improvement is a reasonable expectation, you must see the benefit derived from attending class each day and enduring the physical and emotional challenge of skill development - and it must in some way be relevant to the direction your life is currently moving.

You are no stranger to this process. You have chosen to attend college because the degree (and the knowledge it represents) is a prerequisite for the career you wish to pursue. If, for example, you have decided you want to become a surgeon, you would spend less time taking classes related to journalism or economics and more time taking classes related to organic chemistry and anatomy. Why? Because the perceived outcome you expect to realize - becoming a surgeon - requires that your academic pursuits are consistent with this expectation. And the intensity with which you believe this to be a realistic pursuit is the intensity with which your behavior will be consistent with your dominant values, thus the formation of the right attitude.

The question I ask is, *do you know in what direction your life is currently moving and the extent to which you must apply yourself in class to ensure that your behavior is consistent with your dominant values*? You have career goals and you have life goals, both short and long-term. Whatever they are, my class must somehow fit in order for you to commit to learning more about the game of tennis. Only you can make this determination. I know that, should learning become an expectation in this class, you will, undoubtedly, face many of the same challenges found in classes more relevant to your major. Self-perseverance is essential to success in the classroom; it is also essential to success on the tennis court; self-discipline is essential to success in the classroom; it is also essential to success on the tennis court; self-motivation is essential to success in the classroom; it is also essential to success on the tennis court; personal commitment is essential to success in the classroom; it too, is essential to success on the tennis court.

It is obvious that for you to learn more about the game of tennis, the tools you bring to my class must be the same you would bring to any other. Which means that if tennis skill improvement is what you desire, then the attitude you bring to class, each day, must be consistent with this expectation.

Having said all this about the importance of attitude development, there are two final points you must consider before deciding what choices you are going to make in this class. It would be an absolute contradiction if I were to give you the freedom of choice - relative to learning the skills I will be presenting - and at the same time do or say anything that would imply that choosing the path of least resistance - pursuing the grade or the credit - is indicative of the wrong attitude. As a teacher, I place the principles of self-perseverance, self-discipline, self-motivation, and personal commitment among life's highest virtues. However, as important as the game of tennis is to me, and my desire to share my knowledge with you, it is just as important to me that you set your expectations for this class - which may or may not include skill improvement - according to your own agenda.

Also, possibly the greatest benefit to be derived from taking this class is having an opportunity to work on attitude development in a non-threatening environment. While the attitudinal and cognitive challenges you must face this semester are the same - both in my class and in others, the consequences for failing to live up to these challenges are not. Achieving success in other classes is often predicated on your attitude being consistent with the preset expectations of your instructor. Any class where your grade is determined by what you learn, and where the subject matter to be learned is inconsistent with your current dominant values, eliminates any viable alternative. This class affords you the opportunity to work on developing the right attitude for goal achievement without fear of reproach, whether you realize your performance goals or not. And I can think of no better means by which to pursue this challenge than by learning more about the game of tennis.

Finally, as you continue to seek personal fulfillment this semester, it is important to remember that your goals and expectations will not be handed to you on the first day of class. They will be set by you according to the relative importance this class has in your life at the moment. In the end, you will find that your success in my class will not be defined by your ability to hit a better backhand. Your success will be defined by the degree to which you more fully understand where your life is going, and the extent to which your expectations are consistent with your chosen path. And it is this self-understanding that will remind you that the game of tennis, like life, is heavily weighted toward having the "right attitude."

PART TWO: SELF-DIRECTION

Chapter 5
Purpose

One of the many things I have come to know about your potential for actualization is that regardless of what may have brought you to my class, everything you experience will have some relationship to your existence beyond its boundaries. You will not experience the game of tennis in a vacuum - the student learning how to hit a better forehand is the same person that will later work on being a better parent or being a more productive worker. It is this knowledge, and my belief that what you experience in class is a means to a greater end, that serves as the foundation of this chapter. As certain as I am that there is a relationship between the game of tennis and the game of life, I am also certain that the quality of what you experience in my class - both in the context of improving your backhand and improving your life - will most accurately be measured by the degree to which you have a sense of "*Purpose.*"

In observing the performance of parents, corporate executives, entrepreneurs, and athletes, I have found three attributes which separate the highly successful performers from the rest. These attributes so closely linked to high achievement are: 1) Responsibleness, 2) Nowness, and 3) Meaning.

Responsibleness starts with the understanding that *everything you experience in life is an achievement, by your own hand and of your own mind.* The result of your effort at work, whether it is productive or destructive, is an achievement. The quality of your relationship with a friend, whether it is good or bad, is an achievement. Your grade in biology, whether it is an "A" or an "E," is an achievement. Your attitude toward life in general, whether it is good or bad, is an achievement. In the context of my class, your grade, whether it is an "A" or an "E," is an achievement. Your attendance, whether you are here every day or only occasionally, is an achievement. What you experience when you attend class, whether you experience fun or frustration, is an achievement. Your level of self-understanding during the course of this semester, whether it is raised or remains the same, is an achievement.

Whatever you experience in my class, whether productive or destructive, right or wrong, directed toward your stated goals, or against them, is an experience you create by means of specific behaviors you adopt. What this says is that during the course of this semester you most certainly will accomplish something. And it is your sense of responsibleness that will determine whether what you experience is by choice or chance, by design or by default.

Since everything experienced with feeling is a self-creation, the measure to which your achievements are what you want them to be will be the measure to which you set your goals. If you are happy at this moment it is because you have, by design, chosen to act in a manner which leads to happiness. If you are unhappy it is because you have, by design, chosen to act in a manner which leads to unhappiness. Thus, if you improve your backhand this semester you will do so because your goal was to improve your backhand. Likewise, if your backhand does not improve it is because you have chosen to act in a manner which hinders improvement.

Goal setting is essential to having a sense of purpose. You already know that everything in life, good or bad, is an achievement. And you know that success is the achievement of something valued. And you also know that a goal is something you aim for by choice. If achievement is a continuous life process, and you wish to achieve only things that you value, then I see goal setting as the sole means by which this can be accomplished. And this is a responsibility which rests with each person for himself. Your life will always be moving in some direction. The question is, *is this direction by your choosing*?

Your academic environment is a great example of goal setting. You have a presumed goal which is the attainment of a degree. To fulfill this goal you must fulfill other goals, such as enrolling in appropriate classes. You must further fulfill the goal of earning passing grades which can only be accomplished by successfully completing assignments and passing examinations.

Suppose you decide to pursue a career in medicine. What chance would you have of succeeding if, when you enrolled in college, you had no idea which classes were required for your undergraduate degree? What if you decided to register for classes purely on the basis of what looked easy or fun, or if biology or anatomy were given no more importance than economics or art? What if you took the correct classes but there was no assigned work, no grading policy, no way of assessing whether or not you had learned the material presented? I am sure you would agree that your chances of becoming a physician would be slim indeed.

In spite of a preponderance of evidence supporting the need for setting goals, I have seen too many students make college a career, and either drop out with no degree or get caught in a continuous loop of taking class after class, with no progress toward a degree. Without a doubt, this is the fate most likely to befall the student who attends college without a defined sense of purpose.

You may find goal setting difficult for two reasons, both of which have to do with the concepts of commitment and failure. How committed would you be toward setting a goal if you knew that no matter what you did, you would not fail? On the other hand, how committed would you be toward setting a goal if you knew that no matter what you did, you would not succeed? Your commitment to attend college is made possible, in part, by your belief that you will be able to earn a degree. Your commitment to a specific major is made possible by your career choice and your belief that you will realize this expectation. How authentic you are to your commitment is tested each day by the prospect of failure. The more likely the prospect of failure, the more likely you are to alter, in some way, your commitment to achieve. Time and again I have seen students succumb to the perception of failure, sometimes resulting in a student changing his career, or, on a lesser level, choosing to take badminton instead of tennis.

Even when you are willing to commit to goals and are not afraid of failure, the likelihood of your setting goals in this class may be affected by your relationship with your classmates. What I have observed in my class is a tendency for a student to allow his behavior to be shaped, not by his goals and aspirations, but by the behavior of his practice partner on any given day. For example, often I will suggest a drill which requires each student to work with a partner for a brief period of time. Because my drills are optional - you may participate to the extent you choose - often a student who might want to participate in the drill to improve a specific skill will yield this desire to the wishes of his partner, even if this means hitting balls with no specific purpose.

What I have observed about goal setting in my class is that, typically, a student will be more inclined to impose his will on his partner in a non-committal way - *the path of least resistance* - than in a manner which would potentially threaten his partner's comfort. Because my class differs from others (you set the standard of performance each day) this means that any goal you pursue will be set and achieved by your own mind. And because this right is shared equally by each of you, this also means that your practice partner, in an effort to achieve his goals, may potentially make it difficult for you to achieve yours. Your commitment to setting and achieving goals this semester must be made with the knowledge that your primary support system will be your own inner desire to grow.

A final reason why you may fail to set goals is that you may not know how, having had little practice in doing so in the past. Look at the manner in which you have learned and continue to learn. While I am unfamiliar with the teaching philosophy espoused in other countries, I am very familiar with the prevailing philosophy of teaching here in the United States, being a product of this system myself. The difficulty former students have had with goal setting in my class lends credence to my belief that, for all its virtues, traditional teaching conditions you to accept, as your own, goals set by others, rather than encourage you to set goals based upon personal ideals and realistic expectations.

For you, success, however defined, has often come about not because of the goals you have set but because of goals that have been imposed upon you. As a college student, your choice of personal goals, in an academic sense, becomes somewhat limited once you declare a major. Your choices become even more limited once you step into the classroom and your instructor dictates what information you must value in order to earn a passing grade. The effectiveness of this system, as I see it, has been and will continue to be measured by the degree to which you learn and follow the rules of the game that you are playing. If you have progressed through earlier schooling earning grades by default, capriciously following a script you have been handed, you may have difficulty deciding what career you want to pursue in college, after all, up until now you have been told what to do and what to think. College, however, affords you, for the first time, the opportunity to choose the direction of your life. Even when you make it past this first challenge, you then may falter once again when it comes to the task of taking the appropriate classes at the appropriate time. The school determines which classes will count toward your chosen degree, and, with sequential classes, when certain classes may be scheduled. Still, if you are not comfortable and familiar with this responsibility, you may not be able to commit to taking the appropriate classes at the appropriate time. That is because, up until now, this responsibility has been assumed by someone else.

You have enrolled in my class for a reason. You may be here because you want to learn more about the game of tennis, or because it is a required elective, or because you need the credit hour, or because of your desire to earn an easy "A." In any event, now that you are here, your eventual success will be based solely upon the goals you set and your commitment to reaching them. If your sense of purpose is limited to earning credit or a passing grade, then your sense of commitment will only be as strong as the prospect of failure, which for my class is very remote. If your sense of purpose is defined by a specified amount of knowledge you wish to acquire, then, too, your sense of commitment will only be as strong as your perceived prospect of failure. The difference between the two - earning credit or a passing grade without intellectual effort, and acquiring knowledge - is dramatic with respect to the challenge you will face each day. Thus, the challenges you will face in pursuit of a grade in this class will not be nearly as threatening, in terms of failure, as those present should you commit to the goal of improving your tennis skills.

Once you know how to set goals, your ability to do so is limited only by your desire and opportunity. I can not control your desire, only you can. I can, however, give you the opportunity to express your desire. The grading policy for this class virtually guarantees you "carte blanche" to pursue personal, worthwhile goals according to the conditions in your life at the moment. Think of it as a blank check for achievement, where you write in the amount. The return on your investment will be measured by the goals you set and the effort you apply. If you want a one hundred percent return on investment then the appropriate goals must be set and sufficient effort exhibited. This works two ways. Depending upon the goals set and effort exhibited, you will either *achieve worthwhile goals by design or unworthy goals by default.*

The importance of nowness to achievement is underscored in the following description of Vitkor Frankl's "School of Logotherapy": "*Live as if you were already living for the second time and as if you had acted the first time as wrongly as you are about to act now*!" Having a sense of purpose in my class means that each class will be a self-contained experience in which your effort or sense of enjoyment of the moment will not be mortgaged for some future expectation.

I recall one day when a student approached me after I had just completed a lecture on attitude development. He asked me if I was always as upbeat and positive as I appeared each day in class and, if so, how was I able to maintain this approach to life. My response to him was that seeing the bright side of life's circumstances came easy to me by virtue of the fact that I considered myself a poor gambler. You see, because I have no contract which guarantees that I will have a tomorrow, I know that any happiness I want to experience can only be experienced *now*. As a teacher, I approach each class as if it were my last, with the attitude that I want my last lesson to be my best.

Throughout the writing of this book, and, in particular, this chapter, I have become increasingly aware of the extent to which we too often subordinate the quality of each moment we live to a past experience or future expectancy. The problem is not so much that we spend time thinking about the past or the future, but that the extent to which we do so prevents us from fully enjoying what we have before us. When I attend class on any given day, there may be any number of events in my life which, relatively speaking, may be disturbing or unpleasant in terms of past performance or future expectation. (Early in my teaching career I can recall giving lectures and on-court instruction, later realizing that while I was physically present, my thoughts were often focused on some past or future event which had little relevance to the immediate task of teaching my students. I can only wonder to what extent this behavior was noticed by my students, as I am sure that my inability to be fully engaged in my work at the moment had some bearing on the quality of my instruction.)

It is important for you to understand how the philosophy I have outlined will impact your skill development. Regardless of the extent to which you develop a sense of nowness, now is the only thing that matters with respect to hitting the tennis ball. The vital question to be answered in the game of tennis is this: *is the racquet contacting the ball in the right place and at the right time in order for it to land where you want it to go?* You may have hit the previous ten balls into the net, yet, if you can learn how to focus on the moment - *what you want to do this time* - it is likely that the next ball will hit your target. As a teacher of sport skills I am convinced that one of the most important factors that will determine how well you learn how to hit a tennis ball is your ability to *keep your mind on what you are doing while you are doing it!*

As your skill improves, so does the challenge and responsibility of present moment thinking. What you have done in the past, right or wrong, has little relevance to what I call the "moment of truth," except that you obviously want to learn from past success and failure. I sometimes refer to nowness as *sticking to essentials*. When you attempt to hit a forehand stroke, *what is required for you to execute the stroke correctly with respect to your target*?

Occasionally I will hear a student remark that his success is limited by his desire to live in the past or in the future. The problem is not living in the past or future, since it is not possible to do either. The problem is using the present moment to lament a past which can not be changed or worry about a future which is not guaranteed. No matter how hard you try to do otherwise, *you can only live now*!

This brings us back to the importance of setting goals. Having a sense of nowness is not possible without a target. And what many students forget is that just as you must direct the tennis ball to a specific target, you must also direct your thoughts and feelings toward a specific target. This target should be the present moment.

This process does not stop with stroke-specific behavior. I have already alluded to the fact that when you attend my class, you will not perform in a vacuum. You will attend class each day with thoughts and feelings which have no apparent or perceived relevance to the game of tennis, yet these thoughts and feelings may have a significant impact on your performance, depending upon whether or not they are appropriate for the goals you have set. In essence, your sense of purpose will determine the extent to which you make it to class, as well as how productive you are when you are here.

A lack of purpose may explain the behavior of a former student named Paul. Paul's attendance was erratic from the very first week. Even when Paul did attend, he often arrived late or left early, and most of the time when he did make an effort to hit balls in class, his enthusiasm and effort gave me the impression that hitting tennis balls was his least concern.

I soon discovered what was negatively affecting Paul's performance. It was after class one day, during a private discussion (which he initiated), that Paul told me about a personal problem he was having at home. It was a family matter involving his relationship with his wife, and much of his frustration stemmed from the fact that he apparently had no one he could share his feelings with. What is important here is not Paul's relationship situation or any resolution which may have ensued subsequent to our talk. What is relevant to our discussion of purpose is the fact that by talking about his problem (I later learned that this was the first time Paul had discussed his problem with someone at school), and allowing me to listen and share my thoughts with him, Paul was able to see how his personal life was adversely affecting his performance in class. When I talked to Paul, I made no attempt to convince him that he could only succeed in my class by disowning or suppressing what was going on in his personal life. As a result of our talk, he gained a little insight about how to positively deal with personal issues without allowing a crisis in one area spill over into another. Just as important was his realization that, personal problems aside, he could still be productive in class by making a more concerted effort to keep his mind on what he was doing while he was doing it.

I know that each of you will have a life to deal with beyond the boundaries of the tennis court. What I do not know is the extent to which you will allow outside experiences to affect what you do in class. As I learned from Paul and other students with whom I have had similar discussions, learning how to stick to essentials will allow you to realize goals in one area of your life even when you are being troubled in another.

When it comes to having a sense of purpose, your understanding of responsibility and nowness is heightened to the degree that you bring *meaning* to this class each day. Occasionally I have been known to ask of a student, "why are you taking my class?" Or, "what meaning have you found in my class?" Or "what meaning have you found in the game of tennis?" As I have come closer to finding the answer to the question of meaning, this process has led me to the discovery that there are two types of people in the world, *those who have discovered meaning and those who have not; the producers and the consumers.*

Meaning describes the essence of our existence which is to seek, at its highest level, self-understanding. Any aspect of our existence outside the self may be viewed as a means to a greater end, not an end in itself. When you have meaning you understand that you are not here to see what you can get out of life, but to see what you can bring to it. A crucial question to ask yourself is, *what meaning does my existence bring to the world*? A man who does not know what he wants out of life is a man who may be looking for meaning in the material world. And if so, he will search for a lifetime and never find it. Meaning, like happiness, can not be found, only experienced. Yet life is replete with examples of how we mistakenly strive for a meaningful existence through external means - what I call a "pseudo meaning". And most often these external means are the efforts or achievements of other people.

A parent who devotes his entire life to raising a son, for example, often validates his existence by his son's accomplishments at different stages of his son's life. This parent experiences a pseudo meaning, one which is fulfilled only to the extent his expectations are fulfilled by his son's accomplishments. Should his son's accomplishments fall short of his expectations, he has no meaning. A person who enters into a relationship with a partner may do so with the idea that meaning can only be fulfilled by displaying unyielding devotion to his mate. Again, this is a pseudo meaning, one which is fulfilled only to the extent that the partner reciprocates. Should the partner at any time prove to be unfaithful, even the pseudo meaning becomes non-existent.

As a coach I witness examples of this pseudo meaning in the competitive arena. A coach who devotes his entire life to developing a champion athlete often validates his existence by his athlete's success on the playing field. His pseudo meaning is fueled by his athlete's wins and starved by his losses.

In the context of my class, you have come here to get something: a grade, academic credit, or more knowledge about the game of tennis. While the first two can be achieved without meaning, the same is not true for the third. Meaning will not be derived from what you get out of this class, but rather from what you bring to it. Meaning will not come from me or what I do for your tennis game. When you experience success and enjoyment this semester, it will be the product of your own thoughts and actions.

I recall a conversation I once had with a private student named Julie. We had just finished a lesson that appeared to be very productive, and I asked Julie to tell me how she felt about her performance the previous hour. Julie was extremely pleased with her performance, citing specific examples of where she had made noticeable progress. She also felt that this lesson was one of her best efforts, emotionally, and proceeded to compliment me for making it such an enjoyable experience. I was in complete agreement with everything Julie said, up to the point where she gave me credit for what she experienced. I was quick to point out to Julie that the enjoyment and improvement she experienced was in no way a product of my effort. Julie brought meaning to the lesson - *enjoyment and improvement were her rewards.*

Julie began to understand that her meaning, and any success derived from this meaning, would be more the result of what she brought to the game of tennis than what the game brought to her.

When you are learning in my class, it is because you bring meaning to your experience. If you are not learning, it is because meaning is non-existent. Likewise, if class is exciting and enjoyable, it is because you have brought excitement and enjoyment to your experience. As with virtually everything else, you have a choice as to whether or not meaning is something you will seek to discover during the course of this semester, a choice I do not wish to subordinate in any way. My final comments on this concept are based upon, and a reflection of, what I have come to know about life and what it means to be a producer - *a man of meaning* - or a consumer - *a man of means.*

When you have discovered meaning, you believe that you are accountable to life, not life to you. You believe that having the means to live by is not as important as having a meaning to live for. And you believe that success is an inside-out process, and that what you get is a manifestation of what you are.

When you have discovered meaning, you will, by virtue of this discovery, become a producer. As a producer, you will know that your success is an achievement exclusive to you; attained through your unique thoughts and actions. You will know that you can not fulfill anyone else's meaning, nor can anyone else fulfill yours. As a parent, you will have meaning whether your child becomes a successful businessman or a criminal. As a woman, or a man, your meaning will be fulfilled no matter how tumultuous a relationship you may share with your partner. As a coach, your meaning will be fulfilled whether your player or team finishes first or last. As a student you will know that success will be defined by what you bring to my class, not by what it gives to you.

You may better understand this philosophy by answering the following question: *if you squeeze an orange, what do you get*? The obvious answer is orange juice. And does it matter who does the squeezing, or how hard? No. You only get orange juice because that is all that is inside. Life works the same way. I know that anything you produce in my class, whether your effort results in success or failure, can only be a manifestation of the thoughts, feelings, attitudes, beliefs, and goals you harbor throughout the semester. I can give you ideas on how to hit a better backhand, but I can not give you a better backhand. I can give you ideas on how to improve your self-image, but I can not give you a better self-image. I can give you ideas about purpose and goal setting, but I can not give you purpose and I can not set your goals. This is to say, I can give you a road map and a set of keys, but you must choose the destination, and only you can drive the car.

Should you choose to not bring meaning to my class, you will, by virtue of this choice, spend your time looking for juice without squeezing an orange. You will be looking for answers from without, never asking questions from within. As a consumer your search for meaning will take you on an external journey which, at best, will culminate in a passing grade or earned credit. As a consumer you will look to me for your salvation as a tennis player, asking me to give you what you do not believe you already have. As a consumer, if you do not get what you want from this experience, you may blame the game, the class, or the instructor, never realizing that what you experience is merely a printout, in full living color, of your life's meaning, or lack of it.

Finally, as you begin to understand what it means to have a sense of purpose you will understand that ultimately, the responsibility for your tennis development rests with you. You must decide exactly what you want from my class. My responsibility is to help you realize your goals by giving you information appropriate to what you desire. Your responsibility is to choose behavior that is consistent with your goal. My responsibility is to help you see where your behavior is taking you. As I continue to promote autonomy as a teacher and coach, I have a growing concern that self-responsibility is not widely taught, nor is it understood as basic and essential for one who seeks personal fulfillment. I am also concerned that, because you may not be ready or willing to assume responsibility for your tennis development this semester, you may, as have many former students, pass this responsibility on to me.

What I find interesting is that you may be willing to put your tennis development in my hands solely on the basis of my being labeled the "resident expert" with respect to my position as a college teacher. The problem is not that you have come to me for guidance. The problem is that you may have come here thinking that I can give you something you do not already have, that I can make you something you do not believe you already are, and that I can take you somewhere you do not want to go or to a destination that you do not even know exists. If this, in any way, is part of your purpose for being here, then it also makes me part of your goal. And if I am part of your goal, you will need to be able to guarantee I would be willing and able to give you what you want, which of course, you can not.

The truth is, even if you tell me what you want (and many students in the past have not), I can not give it to you. Everything I give you in my class comes from my perspective and my values, which may differ vastly from your own. You and I will never see the game of tennis the same way. Suffice it to say, we will never see your development the same way. No matter what I say in class, if you put your game in my hands, *I can only take you where I want you to go*, whether it is in the direction of your goals or not.

Your success this semester begins and ends with purpose. Everything you do this semester will be done for a reason. And because everything you experience will be an achievement, your success will be determined by the degree to which you bring meaning to my class and establish worthwhile goals to ensure that personal fulfillment will be realized. And once you bring meaning to my class and to life in general, you will no longer need to pursue an elusive goal called success. You are success.

Chapter 6
Motivation

In the previous chapter we discussed the importance of knowing what you want from this class and how important it is to your success that this class have some meaning to your existence. You have a reason for being here - you want to learn new tennis skills or improve your existing skills, but having a reason for being here is only part of the process. Now that you are here, any goal you set will be pursued to the degree you can answer the question, *what's in it for me?*

I have already established that everything you do you do for a reason. And I have also established that action, taken by design, is purpose. " *Motivation*," the focus of this chapter, is the means by which you measure the intensity with which you actively move in the direction of your goals. In this chapter I will talk about what it means to be motivated, where it is derived from, and how motivation will affect what you get from my class.

I recall a recent experience which says a lot about motivation and what will be discussed in this chapter. In addition to coaching and teaching I also work part-time as a professional tennis umpire. In late August I work at the US Open Tennis Championships in New York City, which (depending upon the tournament dates) occasionally conflicts with the first week of class. This particular semester I was able to meet my students on the first day where I explained that I would be going to New York and that class would resume in two weeks. Upon returning, I noticed that one student listed on my roster who failed to attend the first class meeting, was still a no show, until four weeks later. His story was that he had been looking for my class since the beginning of the semester and was not able to find any information about its location or when instruction would begin.

When I told Bill I had been out of town and that class resumed in the third week of instruction, and that he was responsible for making up lost attendance points, he felt that he should not have been penalized for missing class. Bill felt that he was not at fault for missing the first day and not finding information as to when and where class would be held. It was easy for me to dismiss Bill's excuse as invalid because attending the first class of the semester was not his only access to the revised start date and location of my class. The department secretary knew my schedule, it was posted on my office door, and it was also detailed on my answering machine.

Bill's desire to find my class was an accurate reflection of how motivated he was to do so. At the time, I may not have known how important my class was to his academic goals, but I did know that the effort he made to find it was consistent with the return he expected on his investment.

Suppose the situation were different. Let us suppose that Bill had been told he had contracted a deadly virus and had only days to find a cure. What if I were the one person who had the cure, and he needed to find me to get it.? How motivated do you think he would have been in this scenario?

I do not know if Bill would have had any more success in finding me in this scenario, but I know that he sure would have tried a lot harder!

Why? Because it would be in his best interest to do so. In either scenario, Bill had legitimate incentive for finding my class. Yes, he was, to some degree, motivated to find his tennis class, but because the incentive for survival is stronger than that of earning a grade, obviously more effort would be exerted toward the former than the latter.

What this says about human behavior is that *everybody is motivated.* It is not possible for you to perform any voluntary function without being motivated to some degree. You do "A" as opposed to "B" because "A" is more important to you. You are "here" as opposed to "there" because you view being here more important than being there. Whether we are talking about your performance as a student, your relationship with family and friends, or your performance at work, everything you do must answer to the question, what's in it for me? This holds true even when doing something for the benefit of another person. Even acts of altruism are, in part, motivated by the anticipated effect your actions will have on others.

The question then, is not *whether* you are motivated, but *by what means are you motivated?* In the previous chapter I alluded to the fact that your role in my class will be that of a "consumer" or a "producer." You are taking my class this semester because of your desire to give something to the game by means of productive activity or you are here because of your desire to get something from it. As a consumer, by design, you will find yourself motivated more by extrinsic means of tangible rewards, whereas, as a producer, also by design, you will find yourself motivated more by intrinsic means or the feelings derived from productive activity.

When you are extrinsically motivated, your incentive to act stems from something you expect to gain or keep and this incentive comes from some external source. You are motivated, for example, by money, by people, and by possessions. In my class you may be motivated by the grade you desire, by the academic credit you may earn, or by the skill you may develop. You may also be motivated by my approval of your effort in class. Extrinsic motivation does work some of the time and under certain circumstances, However, there are limits to the effectiveness of external motivation which I will deal with a bit later.

When you are intrinsically motivated, you are motivated more by the feelings which may accompany a particular act than by what this act will bring you in the way of an external reward. The saying that "success is its own reward" may be appropriate here. In other words success is more in what you feel than in what you get. In my class you may be motivated by the increased self-confidence experienced by achieving worthwhile goals during the semester. You may be motivated by the opportunity to improve your self-concept by accepting a new challenge.

Without question, I am sure you will agree that most people are motivated more by external means than by internal means. This is to say most people are motivated more by objects than by feelings. We live in a society where we make value judgements about what a person is by what he has. And to the degree that we believe this is the way things should be we become driven to act, not by internal gratification or self-satisfaction, but by what we can get and whom we can impress.

Face it. Tangible rewards are much easier to measure and often more easily realized. One method I have used in the past to test this theory is to have students compete against me for points toward their grade. I would initially tell students that any request to hit tennis balls with me would be honored (with no mention of points). I also encouraged them to play games against me so that they could learn more about tennis scoring and improve their skills in the process. Rarely would a student ask to hit with me under these conditions. Most would only do so when I told them that each point they won would count toward their grade. All of a sudden students were lining up on my court as soon as they arrived in class! Not necessarily because of what they could learn, but to win points toward their grade. With few exceptions, I found that most of my former students were more likely to be motivated by a dangling carrot which could be seen, than by one which was only felt.

My grading system also tests this theory. Because my grading is based upon point accumulation, many students complete their grade requirements well before the end of the semester. Some students continue to attend class even though their desired grade is earned. This behavior is typical of a student who may enroll in my class for a grade, but one who also wants to improve his tennis skills. And as long as class is being held, this student knows that he can work on his skills, and will do so. Because the only tangible rewards offered in my class are the credit and the grade, I know that this student's continued effort is the result of intrinsic motivation.

There are some students, however, whose attendance will stop immediately upon reaching the magic number required for their desired grade. Because these students are motivated by the grade or credit, once the reward is reached, a reason to attend class no longer exists.

Lecture days provide further opportunity for me to observe which students are motivated by their desire to learn more about the game of tennis or by a grade. Even though the lecture material I present is an important supplement to the on-court experience, many students fail to share my enthusiasm for these discussions. Because of this, it is not uncommon for attendance to drop dramatically when we are forced indoors because of inclement weather. Even some of those who decide to attend the indoor sessions make it clear (by doing homework for another class, as an example) that their primary reason for attending is to earn attendance points. My attendance numbers do go up, however, when I occasionally double the point value of an upcoming indoor session or when the end of the semester is near and students find themselves in need of a lot of points in a short amount of time.

Occasionally when we meet indoors I substitute a lecture with some indoor drills that can be done using a gym floor and wall. Again my students reveal the source of their motivation. Many students attend these sessions with tennis racquets, prepared to hit tennis balls. A few decide to take the day off since there will be no additional points awarded for a lecture, and hitting tennis balls on a gym floor without a net is not considered "real tennis." Other students, however, attend class, and once they discover what we will be doing, they often participate reluctantly or make the last minute decision to leave or sit and do homework.

Here, the reward of a grade is not the issue. It is the student's motivation being linked solely to the physical act of hitting tennis balls on a tennis court. Speaking from personal experience I can tell you that a lot can be learned about tennis without the use of a tennis court or net. I hit my first tennis ball in January of 1973 in a beginning tennis class at a school that did not have tennis courts, indoor or outdoor. The first two months of my tennis life consisted of hitting tennis balls against a wall off of a gym floor. It was two months before I saw my first tennis court and here I am today, a tennis teacher of more than twenty years. I had little choice but to find a source of motivation linked to something other than hitting tennis balls on a real tennis court, so I chose to look for some not-so-tangible rewards, given the existing conditions.

If tangible reward is your primary source of motivation, you may find it difficult to be motivated to improve when class is indoors. Motivation to improve may also be a problem when, because of the class size, you must share hitting space with other students. You may find motivation toward improvement difficult when you do not approve of the tennis balls I provide for practice. You may also find motivation toward improvement difficult when you attend class, and your usual hitting partner does not. The litany of reasons as to why you may find motivation toward improvement a challenge becomes endless once tangibles become your primary means of being motivated.

Another form of extrinsic reward common to my class and other performance arenas is the use of people as sources of motivation. When my students do class evaluations at the end of the semester, the statement most consistently repeated when asked to list my greatest strength as a teacher, is that I am a great motivator. My concern over this belief held by some students is so strong that each semester, when I talk about motivation and my role as a teacher, I make a point of explaining that the last thing I want is for my students to look upon me as a source of motivation. It is no secret that motivation is one of the essential factors which will determine the degree to which any worthwhile goal will be achieved. And because motivation is so important to successful performance, I want each student I teach to be motivated to learn and improve for personal reasons, not because of who I am or what I represent.

The extent to which an individual is willing to subordinate the responsibility of motivation to another person has concerned me for some time. This is particularly evident in the field of academe. No longer is it enough for teachers to provide information, support, and a positive learning environment. Now, many students expect teachers to be the impetus behind their effort. I find it interesting that I cover material in my class that is worth fifty dollars an hour at my club, yet for many students, I am still expected to motivate them to learn when they attend class.

To help you understand why my role as a motivator should be minimized, let me remind you that the primary reason you are motivated is that you have discovered something you would rather do than not do. This is to say that you are always motivated, to some degree, to fulfill a personal need. What are your needs in this class? Remember, my class is designed to give you a wide range of choices regarding expectations. You may be here for a grade, for exercise, for academic credit, for full time status, or any other reason that may surface. And on any given day your expectations may be high or low, depending upon the outcome you may perceive. How can I, or any teacher, be expected to be a locus of motivation for the fulfillment of needs that may change from day-to-day, and that may be different from student to student?

One important thing I have learned as a teacher is that I can not motivate a class. Each of you will have needs you want fulfilled which will vary in scope and intensity. Only you will know what you want at any given time. Only you will know how important these needs are at any given time. If you look to me for motivation, and I do not provide it, it will be difficult for you to be productive.

Another point which must be considered here is the fact that if I am your source of motivation, *I can only motivate you according to my expectations*. Obviously, since I am here for reasons similar to your's - to learn (although in a slightly different context) - it would be natural, and certainly in my best interest as a teacher, to expect you to be here for the same reason. As a teacher, I am expected to provide ideas and information that will challenge your intellect and stimulate personal growth. This is fine for students who are here for the same reasons. If, by chance, you are here for other reasons, then much of what I may have to offer will have little effect on your goal attainment.

We can look at extrinsic motivation in a different academic context and find that the inherent virtues as well as problems are relatively the same. I recall discussing motivation and academic achievement with some of my students one semester, and I asked one particular student how much effort she would put into her studies and how much she felt she would learn if she did not have to be concerned with grades. Interestingly enough she said that she would probably work harder and definitely would learn more. She went on to say that the pressure of having to achieve grades to graduate caused her to place a greater premium on memorization than on learning subject matter. For me, this was not a new revelation. Early in my teaching career, I sensed that the academic environment as it exists today, for all its virtues, often makes it difficult for students to be motivated intrinsically. That is because the system as we know it can not accommodate the individual needs of each student. As a result, for survival, students must resort to such means as memorization to ensure that the academic expectations of their instructors are met, even at the price of long-term retention.

As you can see, tangible rewards are widely used by students to succeed in the classroom, and this source of motivation (at least temporarily) has, for some, been effective. The problem with tangible rewards is that they are only as effective as they are present or measurable. Many of my students have only attended class to the extent that their effort would be rewarded with a specific grade. Tangible rewards, when used exclusively, can actually cause a decrease in productive performance. An example of this may be seen in the behavior of Pam, a member of my tennis team. As a high school senior Pam was not highly recruited. Also she did not make much of an effort to market herself to prospective colleges and as a result made a late decision to play for my team. Because most of my financial aid was committed for the season I was only able to give her a nominal amount of aid in her first year. Pam was not impressed, and made a point of letting me know that in order for her to compete the next season she would need more money. Because of other recruiting obligations the following season, I was not able to increase Pam's scholarship. And sure enough, she refused to play that season, just because I did not honor her request for additional financial aid. Even when I increased her aid in subsequent seasons, the pattern had been established; Pam's motivation for playing tennis in college was closely tied to the amount of financial aid she would receive. Needlessly to say, this concern over money affected Pam's tennis performance. My efforts to help her with her performance goals were never appreciated, because our conversations would inevitably shift to the issue of money, and how she would work harder on the court if I would give her more money.

While extrinsic motivation has its merits, it is also self-limiting. Once you become accustomed to extrinsic rewards, it can become addictive. You will, over a period of time, convince yourself that you can not perform without the external carrot dangling before you. Another self-limiting factor with extrinsic rewards is that this form of motivation is as much a measure of someone else's expectations as a measure of your own individual effort. This means that the degree to which you sustain motivation toward a specific goal will often be controlled by the degree to which this form of reward is present at any given time. If you are taking my class for a grade, then you will be motivated toward that goal to the extent that it is in front of you. When it is achieved, you no longer have any incentive to continue to perform. *You can not pursue that which you already have.*

Tangible rewards will not be a primary factor in your success this semester, unless, of course, your primary goal is to get a passing grade. Each semester I manage to find a new carrot to dangle in front of those students who seek nothing more than a letter grade or academic credit. At the beginning of the semester you will be given several options for earning points toward your grade. And if you have taken my class before, you will know that it is a common practice of mine to create new opportunities for you to earn points during the semester. These rewards may bring you to class. However, alone, the lure of points will not be enough to help you experience long-term improvement.

Tangible rewards, self-limiting as they are, are merely the means by which you choose to fulfill your need for stimulation. The lure of a passing grade or academic credit may be part of the reason you are taking my class, but something more important to you may be your desire to have fun by engaging in a stimulating activity such as tennis. It is here that your source of motivation becomes more intrinsic than extrinsic. When you are motivated intrinsically, you are motivated to do something because it meets some internal value such as pleasure. This class will be pleasurable to the extent that the challenge of learning the skills of tennis will keep you stimulated at an appropriate level. If, for example, the drills and exercises I present to the class do not challenge your existing skills, you may find yourself under-stimulated, and unable to enjoy the experience. Conversely, if these drills present too great a challenge for your existing skills, you may find yourself over-stimulated, and again, unable to enjoy the experience. Ultimately, whether you experience low stimulation - boredom, or excessive stimulation - anxiety, you will probably find yourself being motivated by some other means, and toward some other goal.

Besides taking my class for positive stimulation, you probably have other expectations, some that are personal and some that are similar to the expectations of other students. All of these expectations, both shared and withheld, will vary in intensity. And because your life does not revolve around tennis (you have other classes which demand your attention) your other needs will influence the effort you will put forth to meet your need for stimulation. You may come into my class with a limited amount of knowledge about how to hit a tennis ball and you may have a strong desire to want to learn more. If this is true, your motivation each day will differ from the student who has limited knowledge about the game and little desire to learn more. You may come into this class with a level of expertise which exceeds the skills I will be presenting and a strong desire to want to learn more. If this is true, again, your motivation each day will differ from the student who has similar skills and less desire. I know that, with few exceptions, most of you will express some desire to learn more about the game of tennis. I also know that the individual needs which accompany this desire will differ.

In the broader context of your total academic experience, your need for stimulation is neither totally dependent upon nor limited to the activities of my class. The classes you are currently taking in addition to tennis will have an effect on how much your motivation is intrinsic. Because this is an elective activity class, it is designed to place the emphasis of fun and enjoyment ahead of intellectual stimulation. By virtue of its academic value - one credit-hour - any need you may have for stimulation will be measured against, and controlled by, the degree to which this need is fulfilled by other classes.

Robert was a student who enrolled in my class with high expectations for improvement. Early in the semester he appeared to embrace the challenge of improving his tennis skills and even mentioned the fact that tennis was his most enjoyable class. Three weeks into the semester, Robert's attendance, participation, and on-court effort continued to be exemplary. He attended lectures and even took notes, and when we were on court he made a sincere effort to challenge himself with the drills I would present to the class, often asking questions about his game and his progress. After five weeks I began to notice a change in Robert's behavior. As we approached the end of the semester his attendance became irregular. Robert often arrived late, and when participating in drills, no longer appeared to have the sense of enjoyment expressed during the first three weeks of school.

It was not until a discussion regarding his grade that I discovered the cause of this change in Robert's behavior. It turns out that he was having difficulty with his other classes which began to affect how he performed in mine. Robert's major was engineering, and this particular semester he was taking five core courses, and each, in its own way, placed excessive demands on his time. Although an excellent student, Robert got in over his head this semester, and became terrified at the thought of not getting an "A" in each of his classes, including tennis. After becoming aware of the outside academic demands facing Robert, I understood why his approach to tennis changed so noticeably. Because of the demands of his other classes, and the self-imposed pressure to succeed, Robert had little left in the way of a need for challenge. The anxiety created by the demands and expectations in his other classes spilled over into mine, which resulted in his diminished desire to embrace the challenge of the game. And because his diminished effort had a negative effect on his physical performance, Robert found it difficult to maintain the arousal level necessary for the activity to be fun.

As you can see, the degree to which you are challenged by your other classes this semester will influence your decision to take my class to learn or just get a grade, and this decision will influence the degree to which your motivation stems from what you can get, or what you can experience.

Each day you may come to class with different goals, and thus, you may have different needs for stimulation. One day you may attend class with a need for stimulation that can only be satisfied by the challenge of learning how to hit a better forehand stroke, yet the next day this need may be satisfied by just playing a game, or rallying, or maybe sitting on the sideline doing homework for another class. Recently I had a student named Carol, who was also a teaching assistant in the Biology Department. Carol had played tennis before taking my class and the grade she received had little to do with her reasons for being there. She enrolled in my class because she had a need for exercise and stimulation that was not being fulfilled through her work as an instructor. Some days Carol would come to class and participate in assigned drills, yet other days she would come to hit a few balls with no specific agenda for improvement. Whatever she did when she was in class, Carol was primarily intrinsically motivated because neither the grade nor academic credit was as important to her as the arousal she experienced hitting tennis balls.

There is another source of motivation which must be discussed, albeit a form of *pseudo motivation.* Often, in an attempt to get a person to do what we want, we do so by means of negative consequences, or evoking the emotion of "fear." I call this form of motivation pseudo because this form of motivation moves one to act more because of what they want to avoid rather than what is desired. As a coach, teacher, student, athlete, parent, sibling, employer, employee, spouse, or friend, we have all at some time been exposed to this form of motivation, either as a perpetrator or as a victim. How often have you, as a student, studied for extended periods without rest, not because of your desire for knowledge but because you fear the consequence of a failing grade?

Most often we are motivated by fear in response to the demands of another person. There are, however, occasions where we are motivated by fear because of a circumstance beyond our immediate control. For example, one story I have heard on more than one occasion is that of a woman who lifted an automobile to save the life of her son. Faced with a circumstance she could not directly control, the emotion of fear - evoked by the thought of losing a loved one - summoned within her an inner strength which allowed her to do something inconceivable under normal conditions. A more personal anecdote I like to tell is about a friend who learned about fear motivation first-hand while in Hawaii on business. Jack was in his hotel room one evening when he heard a noise at his door. Not expecting any visitors, he soon discovered that he was about to be the victim of a burglary, and possible assault. Jack was a small-framed man and he did not have a gun or any weapon to protect himself, so, overcome by fear, he barricaded himself in his bedroom by shoving a cabinet against the door and called hotel security. Once security personnel had arrived and the intruders had left, Jack tried to move the cabinet he had placed against the door but was unable to do so. To his surprise and the surprise of security personnel, a cabinet that was moved quite easily moments earlier by one small individual motivated by fear, now, under normal conditions, could only be moved by the efforts of two, much stronger, individuals.

Both situations, the lady lifting the automobile and Jack moving the bedroom cabinet, serve to illustrate how fear motivation often allows us to summon an inner-strength which, under normal conditions, may not be recognized or thought possible. In both examples, a dangerous situation had a positive out-come because of the beneficial effect of fear as a source of motivation.

Under certain circumstances, such as those depicted above, you can easily see the virtues of using fear as a source of motivation. When faced with conditions as extreme as potential loss of life, motivation by fear is often the only option you are aware of at the present moment. My concern with the use of fear as a source of motivation, however, has more to do with the consequences you must face when this form of motivation is used intentionally; *whether you are the perpetrator or the victim.*

Before I discuss the problems inherent in fear motivation, it is important that you understand some of the reasons we often behave in this manner. First, *fear motivation works.* For all that it may not do, when you evoke fear in a person you are attempting to motivate, you certainly get his attention. Right now you know that you have a choice as to whether or not your grade in tennis is based upon how many tennis balls you hit over the net. Suppose, however, mid-way through the semester you were on target to get an "A," spending most of your time in class socializing with friends, not paying too much attention to how many balls you were hitting over the net, and all of a sudden I told you that the grading policy had been changed, and that your grade would be based solely on performance? Would this get your attention? Would this affect your behavior the remainder of the semester? What if you were on academic probation and in order to avoid being dropped from school and losing your financial aid, you needed an "A" in this class?

When you are motivated by fear, *your attention is immediately heightened.* On more than one occasion I have had a student go through the motions in my class totally oblivious to his progress, only to be awakened by the reality that he has missed four weeks of class, and has only two weeks remaining in which to make up the points in order to pass. Up until now, attending class was viewed almost passively, and maybe an interruption to his day. Now, faced with the possibility of failure, he has become more aware of his attendance, and what he must do to get his desired grade.

Second fear motivation is *convenient* in the sense that fear is often the only source of motivation we are aware of at a given moment. A child is most often a victim of this form of motivation. In my own home, I will negotiate with my wife to get her to do something, and in the next instant, tell my son to do it "or else!" Why? While there is a chance that fear might work with my wife, it is more logical to assume that we can negotiate our way to a solution. With my son, however, logic is not yet a tool within his grasp, which makes negotiation unlikely. Therefore, while it is not necessarily desirable to motivate by fear, there are occasions where I might find it to be an appropriate alternative. In other words, convenient.

To say that motivating by fear is born out of convenience is not to dismiss the fact that convenience is just another way of saying one has little desire to look for alternatives. I find this especially true in the coaching profession, where coaches often use fear tactics to motivate athletes to perform. Coaches who use fear to get their players to respond have substituted emotion for reasoned-judgement, something I will discuss in more detail in a later chapter. Because fear motivation is convenient, grabs one's attention, and often works (temporarily at least) in the eyes of those who use it, the end often justifies the means.

Fear motivation does work, but not without consequences which will significantly impact your tennis development. One of these consequences - the tendency to focus more on the penalty of failure than on the reward for success - will be discussed in detail in chapter nine where I deal with emotions. The consequence I will deal with here is the fact that this form of motivation causes you to respond in the appropriate manner to the extent that the fear element is present. Remember, when you are motivated by fear, you are not driven by what you desire, but by the avoidance of the consequences of *not doing what is expected of you.*

There was a time, early in my coaching career, when I used to make my players do drills in practice which they did not like. I would tell an athlete what I wanted him to do and at the same time tell him what the consequences would be if he did otherwise. And sure enough, he would respond to my wishes, as long as I was standing around, watching his every move. Any time I would temporarily leave the practice site, like clockwork, he would resume doing what he had been doing prior to my request. As much effort as he would put into my drills when I was present, an equal amount of effort was put into doing just the opposite when I was absent, because once the fear element had been removed, so had his incentive to do what I wanted him to do.

In an academic context, ask yourself if the effort you put forth in other classes is more the result of your desire to achieve success or your desire to avoid the consequences less effort would bring? If you seek to acquire knowledge in a particular class, then cheating on an assignment or an examination will not be an option for you. If, on the other hand, you are just seeking a grade, and you fear that there is a chance this goal will not be realized, then cheating is an option you will exercise if you perceive that the consequence of doing so is absent.

As I have come to learn more about motivation and the use of fear, I have also seen how this source of motivation is frequently self-imposed. I continue to observe this phenomenon in some of my students even in the absence of any actions on my part which one might expect from a teacher. The most defining characteristic of my class is the freedom you have to pursue the game of tennis according to your individual needs and expectations. Tennis skill improvement is required only if you choose this grading option. Even under these conditions, a student will find himself motivated by fear; not of me or a potential failing grade, but of a fear of failure in terms of learning more about the game.

The greatest challenge you will face this semester will not come from my expectations or demands. It will come from your ability to be motivated by your desire to improve rather than your fear of failure. Whether fear motivation emanates from within, or is imposed upon you by me, the pathology is the same. If you are motivated by fear of failure, your effort will inevitably be focused more on avoiding what you do not want than in pursuing what you do.

Take the case of Aaron. Aaron started out in my class with modest expectations of success. He had played tennis a few times prior to taking the class but had not been exposed to any formal instruction. Initially he appeared to be highly motivated to improve his tennis skills, enthusiastically participating in the on-court drills I presented during the first few days of class. I did notice, however, that as the drills became more challenging to Aaron's existing ability, his motivation appeared to shift from that of desire, to that of avoiding the consequences of failure. Even though his tennis skills were limited when class first began, the drills I introduced to him were so basic that the possibility of failure was minimized. Soon, however, as I began to introduce drills that required more physical and mental effort (which also increased the possibility of failure), Aaron's response to the new challenge was the same as a student who would choose to cheat on an examination they did not want to fail. He lowered his expectations for improvement, and, rather than participate with the goal of learning more about the game, he now became comfortable with doing just enough to get by and receive a passing grade.

Each of you will, without a doubt, be motivated to achieve. You must decide whether you will be motivated to acquire more knowledge about the game of tennis or to achieve a passing grade. You must then decide whether you will be motivated from within or from without, and further, whether your source of motivation will be based upon what you desire, or what you fear. As a student, while you have the freedom to choose your academic goals, you may not enjoy this same freedom to choose the means by which you will be motivated to achieve them.

One thing you will learn from this class, which is also corroborated in life experiences, is that freedom does not come without responsibility. You will be given the freedom to choose what you want from this class, whether it is just a passing grade or skill improvement. If the grade is what brought you here, then I accept the fact that the grading requirements I impose upon you this semester are not within your control. Even here, however, it will still be incumbent upon you to assume the responsibility of being motivated in a manner appropriate to the grade you desire. As past experience has shown, the task of attending class on a regular basis can become an arduous challenge when your source of motivation is unclear or inappropriate. This explains why so many students in the past, accustomed to being told what they must do, find themselves, as the semester draws to a close, in desperate need of points in order to receive a passing grade. The residual pathology of fear motivation is that it is easy for you to become conditioned to the point where, when the choice to perform or not rests solely with you, a state of paralysis makes it impossible for you to perform productively. Because the grade you desire is only an end to which your attendance is the means, your attendance will be maintained only to the extent you are able make this connection day-to-day. It is likely that, under these conditions, a student may forget he is even enrolled in my class. On more than a few occasions a student has enrolled in my class, attended for a few weeks, and then mysteriously disappeared, suddenly realizing the semester was coming to a close and he was on the verge of failing a beginning tennis class. If the grade is your goal, then you must balance this freedom with the responsibility of finding the appropriate source of motivation to ensure its achievement.

While there may be little reason to be concerned with the element of fear if a passing grade is your highest aim, the same can not be said if you decide that you want to learn more about the game of tennis. You are once again given the freedom to choose the degree to which you will pursue knowledge in my class. And again you must be willing to accept the responsibility of deciding how much effort you will apply toward this endeavor. Learning is a continuum upon which you will be responsible for acquiring new knowledge, reinforcing this knowledge, and acquiring still more knowledge. And every step along the way you will be exposed to the possibility of failure. How you handle this process will depend upon how you are motivated; will you be driven by *fear* because you *have to* learn, or will you be driven by *desire* because you *want to learn*?

Think for a moment of the number of opportunities you have had to choose a worthwhile goal, with this choice, and the degree to which it is realized limited only by your desire. Were you to closely examine your current situation as a college student, you would see that while you are given some freedom to choose your goals, the same can not be said about the means by which you will be motivated to achieve them. Any class you may be taking in which the grade you earn is used as a measure of your success will make it difficult for you to be motivated solely by your desire to learn. Because the value of a letter grade is, in part, based upon the goals and expectations of the instructor, and because the value you attach to the subject matter to be learned is unique to your goals and expectations, some form of compromise as to what will motivate you will be necessary, if you are to achieve your goal (knowledge) and the teacher's (the letter grade). I have designed my class to ensure that this form of compromise will not be necessary. If you are to learn anything more about the game of tennis beyond what you know at the present moment, it will be by your own desire that you will do so. I have succeeded in creating a learning environment designed to not only make it possible for you to learn by means of desire motivation, but one which makes desire motivation necessary.

I have said we spend much of our lifetime striving to perform up to or in accordance with standards set by other people. As a parent, child, teacher, student, employer, employee, or spouse, rare is the occasion where you are allowed to actualize by your own mind and for your own sake. It is because you may have had so little practice that I know, in the context of learning, this class may be one of the most challenging you will experience. Each day you alone will determine your destiny. If your backhand stroke improves, it will be primarily by your effort that it will improve. It will improve because of your desire to do what is necessary to experience improvement, because doing what is necessary is more important to you than doing anything else at the moment. Should you desire to remain at your existing level of ability, this too will be by your effort. You will stay the same because of your desire to do what is necessary to stay the same, because doing what is necessary to stay the same is more important to you than doing anything else at the moment.

Desire is the most authentic means by which you can be motivated. With it comes the responsibility of autonomy and the consequence of personal-fulfillment. My gift to you this semester is the opportunity to understand the concept of motivation, and to discover in a hands-on and non-threatening environment, why you do the things you do. Everything is done for a reason. You have decided to pursue the game of tennis for a reason. You are taking this class for a reason. And having read this chapter, you are now ready to answer the question, *what's in it for me?*

Chapter 7

Obstacles

Much has been written about the importance of goal setting as a means of actualizing your potential. In the chapter on purpose I devoted a considerable amount of effort extolling the virtues of having a plan of development to ensure your success in learning more about the game of tennis. Now that you know what you want as a student of the game, and what is required in the form of desire and motivation to achieve it, I must turn your attention to the final step in the process of self-direction, which is knowing and overcoming the "*Obstacles*" that stand between you and your goal. I have read many instructional books on tennis, many of which have addressed the concept of goal setting as a means of achieving success. What I have not found, however, is a book which discusses in sufficient detail, the obstacles which will affect your goal attainment. As you read this chapter, you will discover that actualizing your potential in this class will become a reality when you first discover what stands in your way.

A few questions which may arise and which will be answered in this chapter are: 1) What are obstacles?, 2) Are obstacles essential to achieving goals?, 3) What kind of obstacles must I recognize and overcome to improve my tennis skills? and 4) If I am only here for a passing grade, with no interest in learning, does this affect how much of an impact obstacles will factor into my success?

An obstacle is anything which stands in the way or holds up progress toward a desired goal. An obstacle may be real or imagined, and it may or may not be within your existing level of awareness. Regardless of the form it takes, an obstacle is something which must be overcome before your goal can be realized.

For example, as a student, you may enroll in a mathematics class because of your desire to learn college algebra. What obstacles will you face here? Learning college algebra will require identification, integration, and retention of information regarding college algebra which you do not already possess. The process of identification, integration, and retention requires that you engage the process of thinking. Because most of the information to be learned will be presented in a classroom setting, your attendance in class will be required. And because your belief system and attitude with respect to expectations do not automatically predisposition you to the learning of algebra, you must choose both the degree to which you believe this goal attainable, and the degree to which your attitude is consistent with your goal.

In a different context, let us say your goal is to drive to New York City from Chicago. What obstacles must be overcome? First, you would need to know how to drive (ability). Second, you would need to know whether New York City is east, west, north or south of Chicago (a sense of direction). And third, assuming this is your first attempt to achieve this goal, you would need to know how to follow highway signs and read a road map (identification and integration of new information).

Whether your goal is driving to New York City or learning college algebra, you must recognize and overcome certain obstacles before your goal can be realized.

The first question I ask you is, *why is there always an obstacle between you and your goal*? Of all the questions I ask my students each semester when discussing goals I consider this to be one of the most important. And I am always surprised by the number of students who fail to answer it. The reason there is always an obstacle between you and your goal is that, *if there was not, it would not be a goal, it would be an accomplishment!* I suspect that the simplicity of this element of goal achievement slips by an inordinate number of students, and if you have ever experienced difficulty in realizing a goal, failure to understand the role of obstacles could be the reason why.

Remember, you are not enrolled in my class because of what you have, you are here because of something you want. Maybe you want to improve your tennis skills. Maybe you just need the credit to graduate. Maybe you are looking to earn an "A" to raise you grade point average. Maybe you are here for intellectual stimulation. Maybe you just want a class where you can have fun in a relaxed environment. Even though I may not know your specific goals, I do know that you are here for a reason. And I know that reason is to get something from my class that you do not already have. And I also know that to get what you want, you must overcome some obstacle to do so.

Regardless of your reason for taking my class, the fact that you must overcome obstacles to get what you want is not within your control. What is within your control is the manner in which you perceive, interpret, and deal with the obstacles you will face. The term obstacle is used to describe every aspect of reality, real or imagined, that may exist between you and your goal. In my study of the relationship between obstacles and goal attainment, I have discovered that obstacles can be described as one of two types - those which are authentic to your goal (essential), and those which are not (non-essential).

Any aspect of reality which can not be violated I consider to be an authentic obstacle which must be overcome. If, for example, your goal is to learn college algebra, you can not change the fact that you must identify, integrate, and retain information relative to college algebra. You can not change the fact that you must attend class with regularity (relative to the amount of information presented in class as opposed to that which can be found by other means). You can not change the fact that you must possess the right attitude and belief system that will promote learning efficacy. These are aspects of reality, with respect to learning college algebra, which I consider inviolable, authentic. In other words, *these aspects of reality are essential to your goal.*

I have further discovered that while there are certain aspects of reality essential to goal attainment, there are others which, at any given time and under any given circumstances, may exist in a perceptual sense which are not essential to goal attainment. These I call *distractions*.

In the process of studying college algebra this semester, you may, at some point decide that you do not like your instructor, or you may perceive an atmosphere of hostility in the classroom because of your ethnicity, or you feel overburdened by the demands placed upon you by assignments from other classes, and allow these conditions to negatively affect your attendance and learning efficacy. While the existence of these aspects of reality are legitimate and, therefore, must be overcome, they are not essential to the goal of learning college algebra. They are distractions.

Distractions are what you see when you lose sight of your goal or you believe your goal is not attainable. While obstacles are inevitable and necessary, distractions are not. When you forget that your goal is to identify, integrate, and retain information essential to learning college algebra, or when you no longer believe this goal to be attainable, the inevitable consequence is that you will, in all likelihood, allow non-essential aspects of reality to become your focus of attention. When you lose sight of your goal, or no longer believe it is attainable, you are more likely to find some condition outside of your volitional control as an excuse for your problems.

With this basis of understanding - you know that obstacles exist, you know how they are defined, and you know that they may or may not be authentic to goal attainment - the remainder of this chapter will be devoted to helping you identify, categorize, and overcome the obstacles you will face in my class.

Bear in mind that, while you have each enrolled in my class for reasons which may differ vastly in scope, you will each nonetheless, face obstacles this semester, and these obstacles will vary in number, type, and intensity, depending upon the goals you may subscribe to at any given time. Because I have taught this class for a number of years with the privilege of being exposed to a variety of interest levels and expectancy sets relative to learning the skills of tennis, I have observed a full spectrum of goals. And this, of course, has allowed me to observe an equal number of obstacles which my students have been forced to identify, categorize, and overcome. While the number of obstacles you may be exposed to is unlimited, I have been able to classify the many obstacles I have observed into the following three categories: 1) Awareness, 2) Attitude, and 3) Work ethic. Everything you achieve, whether you achieve success or failure, will, in some way, relate to what you see, what you feel, and what you do.

You know that awareness is knowledge, and that you can not consistently perform outside the limits of what is known to you at any given time. Awareness can become an obstacle to your success when you attempt to violate this aspect of reality. I find myself having to remind students all the time that, *you only know what you know.* When you perform within the range of your existing knowledge you are telling me that, *you know what you do not know.* And when you attempt to perform outside your range of existing knowledge you are telling me that, *you do not know what you do not know.*

I refer to the example of your desire to learn college algebra. The requirements of identification, integration, and retention are not self-evident, nor do they emerge automatically at the appropriate time. Even though you may bring these skills to class each day, you must decide what and how much information is to be identified, integrated, and retained. The degree to which you fail to actively engage any one of these processes is the degree to which it becomes an obstacle. And you can not actively engage any process which falls outside of your existing range of awareness. Because attending class is required for you to identify, integrate, and retain information essential to learning college algebra, and because attendance or non-attendance requires a decision on your part, you must decide each day if attending class is essential to your goal. The degree to which you fail to attend class is the degree to which attendance becomes an obstacle. You will not attend class if the relationship between attending class and learning college algebra falls outside of your existing range of awareness. Because believing you can learn college algebra and having the "right" attitude are not self-evident qualities which emerge automatically, you must decide whether or not you can learn college algebra and what attitude is essential to the attainment of this goal. The degree to which your belief system and attitude are inconsistent with your goal is the degree to which they become obstacles. Your belief system and attitude will remain inconsistent with your goal if the relationship between what you believe, what you think, and what you want falls outside of your existing range of awareness.

Limited awareness becomes an obstacle when you fail to see what is between you and your goal. This is just as true for your desire to learn college algebra as it is for your desire to succeed in my class. The following stories will illustrate this point.

Take the case of Barbara, a student enrolled in my class three years ago. I have mentioned that I always start each class with an on-court evaluation of the existing tennis skills of each student. During this evaluation, I assess the collective skill level of the class by observing each student while they are hitting tennis balls to a partner across the net. And I ask them to do this exercise armed only with the knowledge of the game they possess at the moment. Recalling Barbara's initial on-court experience, I could not help but notice that she was having great difficulty hitting the ball over the net. Time and again she would swing at the ball only to find most of her shots landing into the net or sailing over her partner's head. In an effort to put an end to her frustration, I pulled Barbara aside and asked her how she was doing. Barbara's reply was, "I can't play tennis, I'm really lousy!" This response did not surprise me. In fact it typified the response often expressed by those students who struggle with the learning process early in the semester. It is also the typical response of a student unaware of one important obstacle to success: *Your ability to achieve a goal is limited by the amount of information you possess relative to its attainment.*

Barbara did not know, at the time, that her knowledge of the game was inconsistent with the outcome she intended to produce. She did not know what she did not know. Regardless of the effort she expended toward her goal, under the existing conditions this effort was in vain, because the obstacle to be overcome - accessing information consistent with the desired outcome - was outside of her awareness.

I spoke with Barbara and explained to her that in order to accomplish the goal of hitting tennis balls to her partner, she would first need to know what was standing between her and her goal. The manner in which she was attempting to complete the exercise was based more upon what she saw other students doing (who had more playing experience) than on her existing tennis skill. At the time Barbara did not possess the tennis skills necessary to fulfill her current expectation. Ability was not her problem. Her problem was that the inconsistency between her current expectation and current ability fell outside of her existing range of awareness. I told Barbara that awareness, in a literal sense, was knowledge, and that knowing better was the first step to doing better. Soon Barbara realized that the indictment of her over all ability was unwarranted, as her performance was a reflection of the existing limits of her knowledge of the game of tennis. Once I explained to her how to hold the racquet, how the angle affected the trajectory of the ball, and how her swing speed affected the distance the ball would travel, Barbara gradually began to experience more success with hitting the ball to her partner. And all that was necessary to make this possible was gaining the necessary information relative to the goal she wanted to achieve.

John was one of the more experienced students in my class, and one of the hardest workers. John rarely missed class and always wanted to work on his skills, especially his serve. His major problem with his serve was that he hit with too much speed and not enough spin to get the ball in the service box. The first time John came to me for help with his serve I asked him what he wanted to improve. He said he wanted a more consistent first serve. I had observed John practice his serve on numerous occasions, and I knew his inconsistency was due to his hitting the ball with too much speed and too little spin. When I asked John what was between him and his goal, not once did he mention his swing speed or use of spin. He talked about his grip, his stance, and his ball toss, but nothing that would indicate that the speed of his swing or the lack of spin on the ball were factors hindering his success. Even with his ability and in spite of the effort he consistently displayed in class, John's serve improved very little during the first few weeks of the semester - because he did not know what was between him and his goal. Some days he would spend an entire class period working on his serve, rarely changing speed or adding spin. Even with my words of advice suggesting that he swing slower and add a little more spin for consistency, John (completely ignoring my advice) continued to experience the same erratic results. It was not until mid-semester that he began to make the changes I suggested, and as soon as he did, John immediately began to hit a more consistent first serve. (John actually came to me later in the semester and told me that he finally realized that what I had been saying was correct. When he knew better, was he able to do better.)

Dan was a student who had played tennis for a period of time prior to taking my class. And because the class this semester had a small enrollment, Dan and I had numerous opportunities to practice together. After the first two weeks, I began playing games against Dan and other students who felt that they were ready to test their competitive skills. I purposefully structured this competitive activity in a manner that would give each student a chance to win points by just keeping the ball in play. Serving was not allowed (the ball was put into play with an underhand stroke) and a self-imposed requirement was that I only hit medium-paced shots down the middle of the court.

Each time that Dan and I would play the results would always be the same; Dan would win a point or two, but he would never win a game. Frustrated by this recurring pattern, Dan finally asked me what he could do to experience more success when we played. I answered Dan's query by asking him if he was aware of the primary obstacle between him and his goal (his goal, I assumed, was to win more points). Dan thought the primary obstacle between him and his goal was poor strategy. He figured that if he played smarter and used better tactics this would increase his chances of winning. To his disappointment this was not the case. Even when Dan changed his strategy - he tried altering the spin on his shots as well as direction and speed - the results remained the same. The reason? Dan simply failed to keep the ball in play long enough to give himself a chance to win more. As often as he changed his game plan, he overlooked the tactic of merely keeping more balls in play. As a competitor Dan felt that the best way to win was to hit winners. Keeping the ball in play and waiting for me to make an error was not an option for Dan because he was unaware that this was his problem. Because he rarely hit more than three shots in the court, his tactics were rendered ineffectual. Dan was not a bad student or competitor. He only knew what he knew. And until Dan would know better, he would not do better.

Your existing level of awareness can become an obstacle to your success even if your goals this semester begin and end with earning a passing grade and academic credit. Take Jill's situation for example. Jill gave every indication from the start that she was in my class for the grade (she needed an "A" to improve her grade point average). She was on probation and was concerned about being dropped from school, and in tennis only an "A" would improve her academic status.

Jill knew from my opening lecture that she could earn an "A" in any number of ways without having to spend a lot of time improving her tennis skills. She knew that her final grade would be determined primarily by her attendance and participation. And participation meant she only had to hit balls with a partner when she was in class; she did not have to make any effort to improve.

In spite of my efforts to make it easy for Jill to realize her goal, she managed to find herself on target for a "C" with only two weeks of class remaining. Jill was surprised at her grade situation, and could not understand why she had so few points so late in the semester. Because her grade was based upon attendance and participation, Jill's unsavory position was the result of missed classes, frequent late arrivals, and numerous instances of attending class without participating. Because she felt a sense of obligation to other responsibilities during the semester, Jill never saw that the one obstacle she would need to face and overcome in my class was attending and participating enough to reach her goal. Fortunately for Jill, she made this discovery before the end of the semester, and within the remaining two weeks of class, she made up the necessary points to earn her desired grade. When Jill knew better, she did better.

The experiences of Barbara, John, Dan, and Jill illustrate a recurring theme in my class: a student's inability to realize his goal primarily because he is unaware of the obstacle standing in his way. In chapter two I discussed the need for desire if you are to increase your awareness. No matter what I do as your coach, it is imperative that you make a conscious effort to know more about the factors which will affect your goal realization. This means you must possess the desire to explore every conceivable obstacle which stands between you and your goal, and decide which ones are essential to your goal and which ones are distractions.

Not only is your existing level of awareness a potential obstacle between you and your goal, but your attitude - what you think about and what you expect - can also become a obstacle. You will each attend class armed with an attitude that is either right or wrong for your goals. Assuming that you know what you want, you must then decide: *are my thoughts and outlook consistent with the goal I am currently pursuing*?

In chapter four you learned that attitude is an active state. It is a reflection and sum total of what you are thinking at any given moment of your life and the manner in which these thoughts are played out in your actions. It is, therefore, conceivable that any difficulty you may experience with goal achievement could be a manifestation of your expectations or outlook, or any quality in between.

For example, I have had many students tell me that they want to improve their tennis skills, yet at the same time profess that "the game is too hard" or "I can't hit the ball over the net." A student will often tell me that he wants to hit a better backhand and at the same time lambaste himself for every unsuccessful stroke and disavow each successful one.

Most often if a student's attitude is his primary obstacle, this is brought out early in the semester, sometimes even in the first outdoor class. Jim was one such student. When he enrolled in my class, I immediately observed that Jim's existing tennis skills exceeded the skill level of all of the other students. It was apparent that Jim had been playing tennis for a number of years, which caused me to wonder what his motive was for taking a class that in all probability would provide little stimulation or challenge.

During the on-court evaluation I told Jim how impressed I was with his tennis skills, and I asked him what he hoped to accomplish during the semester. Jim said his footwork was "bad" and that he needed to work on his "concentration". While I did not agree with his description of his footwork ("bad" was an assessment based upon a comparison to someone else's ability, not his own internal standard), I could see during the evaluation that his performance would improve with more efficient movement.

Even though Jim would be practicing with classmates of a lesser skill level (advanced beginners), I knew that he would still benefit from my drills. Advanced beginners always need to work on movement skills and concentration because they are less skilled in predicting where their partner's shots will land. By participating in the drills Jim could expect to see noticeable improvement in his performance.

Jim did not view the experience in the same way. Watching him during the evaluation I sensed that Jim feared that he would not get the challenge he felt necessary to achieve his goals of improved footwork and concentration. As he moved from court to court hitting with different classmates, he seemingly became more dismayed and appeared to care less and less about how he moved and where he hit the tennis ball. Jim knew that his skills exceeded those of his classmates. And rather than create challenges consistent with his abilities, he became content with abandoning his goals, and with performing in a manner more in line with the skill level of his practice partner.

Jim set the tone for his attitude on the very first day and it was played out in similar fashion throughout the semester. Jim had trouble experiencing the improvement he desired because his outlook, and thus his expectations, were inconsistent with his stated goals. Jim's troubles had little to do with his ability or knowledge of the game; he had been playing tennis long enough to know what was necessary to reach his goals. Jim mistakenly assumed that he could only improve his skills by practicing with a partner with similar or better skills. From past experience I knew that Jim could work on achieving his goals with almost any student in the class if he approached the situation with the right attitude. Jim, however, chose to use the situation he faced as an excuse for his pessimistic approach to class each day, and for the abandonment of his goals. It was clear that his attitude was the first obstacle which needed to be overcome. Unfortunately Jim never overcame this obstacle. Even as he became aware of his outlook and lowered expectations, knowing his attitude needed to be changed was not enough to make it happen.

Occasionally a student with the wrong attitude will decide that the obstacle between him and his goal is either me, as his instructor, or his classmates. Such was the case with Tony. Tony, much like Jill, was taking my class because he needed the academic credit to maintain full-time status as a student in order to keep his financial aid. Learning more about tennis was not a priority for Tony because he had taken lessons and practiced on his own outside of class. Tony also knew that to pass the class and earn the academic credit, he would need to attend class and participate on a regular basis.

Tony had two problems. One, he did not enjoy practicing with his classmates. It was a beginning class and no one in the class possessed the skills to give him the workout he desired. As a result, Tony often missed class or did not participate when he did attend if he could not find a suitable practice partner. Two, Tony had no interest in my lectures. While I only gave five lectures during the semester, the point value of each lecture was much higher than the other on-court classes.

Students were not required to take notes and there was no test on the lecture material, however, students were required to attend each lecture on time and stay for the duration to receive the points. Tony did not want to be bothered with lectures on tennis. This I could tell by his falling asleep during my first discussion. It did not take long before Tony decided to skip the lectures completely, forfeiting the points he could have earned toward his grade.

Because Tony stopped attending the lectures (they were boring), and because his attendance and participation became erratic even when class was held at the courts (he did not enjoy practicing with his classmates), he did not earn enough points to get a minimum passing grade. Tony used my lectures and the skill level of his classmates as his reason for failure. The truth is, Tony failed because of his approach to the class in terms of outlook and expectations. He failed to see that if academic credit was his goal, and if the requirement for this was attending class and hitting a few tennis balls, then having the "right attitude" would have meant viewing the lectures and on-court situations as essential to the achievement of his goal. Tony could not do better because he did not know better. He only knew what he knew.

Paul enrolled in my eight o'clock class which met four days a week. He took this class because he needed the academic credit and a high grade, and my eight o'clock section was the only one which fit his schedule. I made my usual opening speech about my grading policy and how a student could easily earn an "A" with regular attendance and participation. I even described how a student could make up points by attending other sections of class, even lectures where the point value was significantly increased. Even with my liberal grading policy, Paul found himself on the verge of failing my class six weeks into the semester.

Paul had several excuses for his precarious situation. One, he blamed the time of the class for his poor performance. For some reason he decided that it was someone else's fault that he was taking an eight o'clock tennis class, not his own. Two, I was seen as part of the problem with his performance. Although my grading policy was extremely liberal, I held a hard line with respect to punctuality. Points were deducted for arriving after the starting time of class and for leaving before I had taken attendance. Paul blamed me for unfairly deducting points from his grade, even though he was the one who often arrived after the starting time of class, or left early or occasionally did not participate when he did attend. Three, Paul occasionally worked nights, and therefore found it convenient to consider his job to be an obstacle between him and his goal of passing my class. Never once when discussing his progress, did Paul acknowledge that the obstacle between him and his goal was his lack of effort to attend and participate enough in class to progress toward his desired grade.

Paul's opinion of an eight o'clock class was not essential to his goal; his decision to take an eight o'clock tennis class was a conscious decision based upon his available options. Paul's opinion of my grading policy with respect to attendance and punctuality was not essential to his goal; Paul had no control over attendance policy. Paul's displeasure with his supervisor's decision to occasionally ask him to work the night shift during the week was not essential to his goal; Paul knew when he accepted the job that working week-nights, on occasion, was a condition of employment.

Paul desired a high passing grade and the academic credit. The only requirement essential to this goal was attending class on time and participating enough to earn the desired grade. Nothing else mattered. But because he never focused on overcoming the obstacles in his way at any time during the semester, Paul was unable to fulfill the requirements for the grade he desired. His success was limited by his awareness. What Paul did not know, he could not overcome. Paul only knew what he knew.

The outlook and expectations you bring to my class will be of critical importance to you if this is your initial exposure to the game. Paula's experience is a case in point. Paula's performance at the beginning of the semester, especially her outlook and expectations, served as evidence that attitude, more than ability, will determine your level of success in anything you do. Paula was an individual who seemed to habitually make a point of looking at the negative side of things and predicting failure even before a task has begun.

I remember the discussion I had with Paula after my introductory lecture on the first day of class. She told me that she wanted to learn how to hit tennis balls with a partner so that she could play against her boyfriend during the summer. She also made a point of telling me how bad she was at tennis. When I asked for evidence to support this belief about her tennis ability she proceeded to tell me that she had never played the game before. Paula's statement about her ability was not based upon past experience as one might expect, but upon a outlook derived from only having observed her boyfriend playing tennis with other people.

Because of her outlook, Paula had set herself up for failure from the start of class. During the on-court evaluation, Paula had a difficult time sustaining rallies with her practice partner, which only added fuel to her conviction that success at tennis was not in her immediate future. Each time a shot was missed, Paula became more entrenched in her beliefs about herself, as inaccurate as they might have been.

Knowing the attitude and low expectations currently embraced by Paula, I knew any expectations I may have held for her insofar as learning was concerned would go unfulfilled. I knew that until she challenged the primary obstacle confronting her - her attitude - there would continue to be an obstacle between Paula and her goal.

In spite of Paula's attitude at the start of the semester, I felt that, in time, she would make the necessary change in attitude which would allow her to realize her goal of learning how to hit tennis balls with a partner. As the semester progressed, I made no attempt to force the issue of learning with Paula. I did encourage her each day, as well as provide her with helpful suggestions as the opportunity presented itself. At no time, however, did I impose any guilt on Paula by telling her that if she would only try harder she would do better. Because she was free to perform at a level of her choosing and according to her expectations, Paula soon began to realize that her troubles had less to do with the game and her effort, and more to do with how she interpreted what she was doing. By her own initiative, Paula began to change her outlook, not necessarily seeing different things, but seeing the same things in a different way. She did not go from beginner to intermediate overnight. She did not learn how to rally with consistency with a partner overnight. And she did not set challenging, yet realistic goals overnight. Paula did, however, make considerable improvement in each of these areas during the last four weeks of the semester. And I attribute her change in performance to her decision to recognize, accept, and challenge the primary obstacle between her and her goal. Paula's attitude was not the only obstacle which needed to be confronted. But no other obstacle loomed as large in importance as the outlook she held and the expectations she set.

Another obstacle which could stand between you and your goal is your work ethic, which is comprised of the following three components: 1) Intensity, 2) Duration, and 3) Specificity. Intensity is the mental and physical effort you apply toward your goal. Often when someone is being described as a hard worker - one who works with great intensity - he is said to have a strong work ethic. While this description is accurate, I also find it to be somewhat incomplete. Intensity is important and necessary but can be wasted if this effort is not sustained, or if it is directed toward the wrong activity. I describe a person performing in this manner as one who is *confusing activity with accomplishment*. Having the "right" work ethic (it can never be good or bad) consists of working on the right thing with the necessary intensity and duration.

Often when a student fails to realize his goals in my class I immediately look at his work ethic to find the reason why. I find that he works hard but not long enough. Or, he works long and hard but not on the appropriate goals. Or, he works on the appropriate goal but without the required intensity or duration. Work ethic is a multifaceted aspect of human performance, and is only as strong as each individual component.

Often a student will tell me he wants to improve his backhand stroke. I will observe him in practice and notice that almost every stroke he hits is a forehand. Now this student could be displaying the intensity and duration to achieve his goal but, unfortunately, because he has chosen to hit more forehands than backhands, his goal may not be realized. If you want a better backhand, the process begins with hitting more backhands.

Intensity is not just physical effort, *it is also mental*. Having the right work ethic means that your focus of attention is primarily directed toward the goal you wish to accomplish. Occasionally a student will experience difficulty realizing a goal in my class because his focus of attention is not centered on the task at hand. For example. On more than one occasion a student in my class has brought a friend to class to watch him practice. As often as I allow this, it never fails that this student will spend more time conversing with his friend than hitting tennis balls. I have even witnessed situations where a student will be engaged in a conversation with his friend at the same time he is attempting to hit balls to his partner across the net. It is obvious that this level of intensity will have a significant impact on his ability to accomplish his goals.

Intensity may also be affected when two students enroll in my class who happen to be close friends and decide to practice together. Whenever Bill and Carol attended class, they would always make an effort to practice together, even if this meant one would have to sit on the sidelines at the start of class until the other arrived. They would go to the same court when possible, and engage in the usual routine of standing at the net talking (usually about something unrelated to tennis) until I would walk by to see if they needed my assistance. As I approached their court Bill and Carol would immediately discontinue their conversation and begin hitting tennis balls - that is, until I would leave. It would take no longer than for me to get to another section of courts before I would observe, from a distance, Bill and Carol back at the net, once again engaged in conversation. On more than one occasion I have found it necessary to remind students such as Bill and Carol that using my class as a social gathering place was not just a potential threat to their grade (participation points are awarded for hitting balls, not talking), but this behavior was an immediate threat to the realization of any performance goals they may have set.

Still another behavior pattern I frequently observe is that of students who often arrive after the start time of class and leave before class ends. A student behaving in this manner would mistakenly believe that he could realize his goals without putting in the time on court hitting tennis balls. I am reminded of Jeffrey, a student who indicated, as did many other students, that he wanted to improve his tennis skills. His actions when he attended class, however, said something different. Jeffrey usually arrived ten to fifteen minutes past the start time of class and rarely stayed until the end.

After the first four weeks of the semester when I began taking attendance half way through the class period, I noticed that Jeffrey would be among the first to leave. Therefore, it did not surprise me that by semester’s end, he had failed to realize his goal. Jeffrey's skill improvement was minimal, in part, because he failed to recognize and overcome the primary obstacle standing between him and his goal. His limited improvement was the result of spending too little time on court hitting tennis balls.

What you achieve in my class, be it success or failure, will be determined by a number of factors, a few of which may be disguised in the form of obstacles. These stories represent many of the students whose problems in my class were more the result of obstacles that were not recognized or overcome, than the result of ability, desire, or knowledge. At the beginning of the chapter I discussed how a student's failure to realize his goals is the result of not knowing which obstacles are essential to the achievement of his goals and which ones are not. This student failed to recognize the difference between an obstacle and a distraction.

As I reflect on the success and failure of former students, I am persuaded that many of those students failed to realize their goals because they focused more on distractions (conditions they could not control and which were non-essential) than obstacles (conditions they could control and which were essential).

Think about your reasons for enrolling in this class. If hitting a better backhand is your goal this semester, what is essential to your achieving this goal? The three essentials you must be concerned with are your awareness (what you know relative to your goal), your attitude (your outlook and expectations), and your work ethic (the effort you display toward the achievement of your goal). Who is teaching the class is not essential. I, therefore, should not be perceived as an obstacle between you and your goal. As long as I provide the information necessary for you to learn more about the game of tennis, nothing else I do should be of concern to you. If I am providing the information your need to achieve your goal, any further attention you give to me or what I present in class is non-essential to your goal of hitting a better backhand. Remember, I am not your goal: a better backhand is.

If you are here for a passing grade, what is essential to achieving this goal? The three essentials you must be concerned with are regular attendance and participation, and (depending upon the grading option you choose) turning in chapter summaries or improving your tennis skills. These are the only three conditions which will affect your goal achievement. The importance of your awareness, attitude, and work ethic may or may not be essential. Where you hit the tennis ball may or may not be essential. What you choose to believe, philosophically, may or may not be essential. What you choose to know may or may not be essential. Any attention you give to me or what I present in class beyond the that which is connected to your desired grade is not essential. I am not your goal: a passing grade is.

In a broader context I have found that students far too often fail to make the distinction between factors which are essential to goal achievement and those which are not. As a student your reason for attending college is to gain knowledge which you do not already possess and to pursue a career goal of your choosing. If this is true (the number of students who start college but never finish suggests that this is not always the case), then what factors are essential to your success? They are no different than the ones I have spelled out for you to succeed in my tennis class. Awareness, attitude, and work ethic are the essential factors you must deal with, and they are the same for any class you are taking. You take a class in organic chemistry because you want to become a physician. Who is teaching the class is not essential. The information the instructor has relative to your goal of becoming a physician is. Over the course of your college career you will probably have a few instructors you will not like for one reason or another. You must ask yourself, *is what I feel about my instructor essential to my goal of becoming a physician*? In all probability it is not. If your instructor is giving you the information you need to achieve your goal, then anything else about him you choose to acknowledge and give attention to is nothing more than a distraction.

Based upon comments made to me by former students, instructors are often considered to be an obstacle to be overcome in the classroom. Yet, based upon personal observation and experience, I believe it is rare that a teacher is a legitimate obstacle in his role as a communicator of information. I find more often than not that a student will falsely label an instructor as an obstacle only because he has temporarily lost sight of his goal. What this says is that your feelings about your instructor have become more important than learning.

If your goal is to become a physician, you must also ask the question, *is it important that I meet with the approval of the person sitting next to me in class*? It is a reality of academic life that you may, from time to time, encounter some form of social intolerance as a college student. is no less apparent in the academic environment than it is in society in general. You can not control this. Yet, too often a student will become so consumed with his need for acceptance that his reason for attending college becomes lost in the process. You need to keep your goal in mind. You are here to learn organic chemistry and become a physician. As long as the person sitting next to you does not infringe upon your right to pursue your goal, how he feels about you personally is not essential. To give this person any attention beyond that which is necessary for you to achieve your goal is to say that being accepted by a classmate is more important than learning organic chemistry and becoming a physician.

I think you get the picture. Your success this semester, in my class and others, will not be experienced without your having to overcome a number of obstacles. The formula for success is simple. You must decide what you want - a grade, knowledge, or something else of value - and then you must discover what is between you and what you want. This discovery is often made difficult by an over-emphasis on your desired goal, with little attention given to the obstacles which must be overcome. Years of experience has taught me that setting goals and keeping them within sight are important steps toward achieving success at any level. What I have learned from teaching this class and researching this book is that it is just as important for you to be aware of the obstacles essential to goal attainment.

PART THREE: SELF-MANAGEMENT

Chapter 8
Learning Efficacy

Until now, I have discussed a number of psychological and metaphysical concepts which help explain why - as a human entity -you behave the way you do. Each concept thus far has served a dual purpose: 1) Helping you set and reach a personal, worthwhile goal, and 2) Providing you with insight - your awareness of the degree to which your behavior is taking you closer to or further away from your goal. And each concept has addressed your performance in my class from the broadest possible context - from your desire to earn a passing grade with minimal intellectual effort, to your desire to increase your knowledge of the game of tennis by means of a personal commitment to skill development.

I now wish to turn your attention to a concept designed to address one specific aspect of your existence which is "*Learning Efficacy.*" Unlike each preceding chapter, where equal validation, and thus attention, was given to your *non-performance* or *non-intellectual* pursuits in my class, here, my sole purpose is that of helping you gain more insight into the process involved in progressing from a base of zero knowledge to that of successfully learning a new skill.

Before proceeding I must state that the implications of the material I am about to present will reach well beyond the boundaries of the tennis court. As this chapter unfolds, you will see that my references to the game of tennis, and the accompanying stories, merely describe the means by which this concept has been played out by former students. Thus, my greater concern lies with the more far-reaching effect of learning efficacy on the totality of your existence beyond my class and the game.

I will begin with a confession. You have probably enrolled in my class under the assumption that I know something you do not. You are looking for new information about the game of tennis, or about learning, or about some aspect of performance that you do not already have, and therefore, you expect me to say or do something that will ensure that you realize your goals. A point which will become eminently clear is that, other than my knowledge of the game, everything contained in this chapter is already known, by you! In fact, I will say that were this not true, and this information were new to you, I know that, literally speaking, it is unlikely that you would be enrolled in my class, or any class this semester.

While it may be true that I have some knowledge of the game of tennis that you do not currently possess, the same can not be said about the process of learning efficacy. The fact that you currently possess a certain amount of knowledge and demonstrated skill is self-evident - the proof is that you are here. What is not self-evident, and thus, needs clarification, is your awareness of the two forces which determine efficacy (your understanding of the process involved in learning), and how you deal with the conditions which affect this process. Therefore, my concern is not with what you know and wish to learn, but with the efficacy which has brought you to where you are.

One of the most exciting experiences of my life occurred in June of 1991 when my son, Leigh, began taking his first steps as a six month-old toddler. He actually may have started before this period, but it was the first time I observed, first-hand, his attempt to experience a new aspect of his existence. This task, however, was not accomplished without some assistance; a sofa, a chair, a wall, and a table leg, were all used at some point to help him explore and expand his world. I do not know what motivated him at this time, and I may never know. What I do know is that for Leigh, as part of his evolution, the time was right.

My reading on the subject of learning has been extensive, as has my writing, yet nothing I have read or written has done more to expand my knowledge of how we learn and perform than what I learned from Leigh during the summer of 1991. And each day that I observe Leigh explore his ever-expanding world, I am absolutely convinced that children are, by far, our most precious resource for understanding both the process involved in learning and the conditions which determine efficacy.

What is learning efficacy? Learning efficacy is *the process of acquiring knowledge and using this knowledge to produce a desired effect.* Before addressing the conditions which affect learning efficacy, I wish to address the process involved in learning a skill, something I refer to as the "stages" of learning. It is the systematic progression through these stages which will determine how well you learn the skills involved in tennis.

This progression is easily understood by the manner in which you learned how to walk. Let me illustrate. When Leigh was first born, his knowledge of his existence and his surrounding environment was very limited. In the context of walking, as a new-born, Leigh was a "unconscious-incompetent." He could not perform the act of walking, and he did not know that he could not walk. As his motor-skills developed, and he became more aware of himself and his environment, Leigh's curiosity fueled his desire to explore different aspects of his surroundings, thus, he began to crawl from room-to-room. As he progressed from crawling to the stage of standing upright and attempting to move in this manner, Leigh became a "conscious-incompetent." The skill of walking was now part of Leigh's existing level of awareness (although not conceptually, but by association). It became something he wanted to do, but he still could not do it. As Leigh's curiosity and motor skills developed further (he became more aware and more skilled), he learned how to use his environment - a sofa, a chair, a wall, and a table leg - to assist him in his attempt to walk. At this stage he found that he could walk, but not without some assistance, and he found himself falling down often if he was not careful to pay close attention to each movement. Leigh had now become a "conscious-competent." He could walk, but he was only successful to the degree that he was fully-conscious of what he was doing. Finally, after weeks of trial and failure, trial and success, Leigh reached the stage of development where he was able to walk, unaided, without having to make each step a conscious act. He had now become a "unconscious-competent." He could walk, and he no longer had to think about walking.

To put Leigh's accomplishment in perspective, I compare his learning the complex motor skill of walking without any instruction or assistance, with a student at my tennis club who pays me fifty dollars an hour once-a-week to learn how to hit a forehand.

Why is it that a child, possessing little in the way of knowledge, experience, and aptitude, can learn at such a phenomenal rate, yet, a student will take tennis lessons for years and never remove the hitch that is plaguing his backhand? Are you born with some unique capacity for learning that somehow diminishes as you grow older? Is it possible for you to turn back the clock, and recapture a skill you once had and apply this skill to learning more about the game of tennis? What is it about adults that often makes learning a new skill an arduous and occasionally traumatic experience? These are the questions this chapter will address, and in the process, show you that one of the most important steps you will need to take to learn more about the game of tennis, is a step backward - a revisit to your childhood.

The fact that you were able to walk to your car or to the train, and that you walked to my class today serves as evidence that the stages of learning I have described have some validity. The exception of course, may be those of you who *crawled* here on *hands and knees*! What will also become more evident as the semester unfolds, is the extent to which your behavior remains consistent with these stages and how this relationship plays out in your ability to learn more about the game of tennis. The following stories will illustrate how some of my former students have attempted to alter the order in which these stages occur, or, in some cases, attempted to bypass one or more of these stages altogether.

Steve was a student whose approach to learning how to play tennis gave me the impression that he apparently forgot how he learned to walk. Steve had played tennis occasionally prior to enrolling in my class, and stated that his goal was to improve his serve so that he could play better against some of his friends. Steve did not have a problem working on his serve when he attended class; he, in fact, devoted a considerable amount of time to this stroke each class period, often arriving early and staying late. Steve's problem was that he would hit his serve too hard and too low to the net for it to consistently land in the correct service box. Even though most of his serves hit the net (with a few landing well beyond his target), Steve allowed the occasional good serve to convince him that he was on target, contrary to feedback given by me or the number of serves hit into the net.

From the first time Steve attempted to hit a serve, power was the most important thing to him. Because of what he observed in other tennis players with more experience he felt that having played occasionally, he should be able to serve like players who had been playing much longer. What Steve failed to realize was that many of the players he attempted to emulate had more experience, and had developed a consistent and accurate serve long before they hit with power. Steve was frustrated with this particular stroke because he was attempting to perform outside of the limits of his existing ability. Steve did not know that a consistent and accurate serve had to be developed before he could hit one with power. Steve was a *conscious incompetent.*

Doug enrolled in my class even though he had been playing tennis long enough that his skills, although still limited, exceeded those of most of the other students. Doug was successful in hitting the ball over the net when he would pay close attention to nuances of each stroke. When hitting his forehand and backhand strokes, he had to consciously be aware of his footwork, stance, and swing, otherwise he would experience difficulty hitting the ball into the proper court. Whenever Doug practiced with a lesser-skilled classmate, he could do moderately well without using much conscious effort, unlike when he would practice with a classmate of equal skill, or with me. When Doug and I practiced together it was apparent that total concentration was needed for him to keep the ball in play because I usually gave him more opportunities to do so than his classmates. Whenever his attention would be drawn to something other than his footwork, stance, or swing, Doug would invariably hit most of his shots into the net or outside of the court. Doug was a conscious-competent.

Chris enrolled in my class for a reason other than learning more about the game of tennis. Chris happened to be a member of the women's varsity tennis team and took my class because she needed a one credit-hour elective course and, having choose to between bowling and tennis (these were her only options at the time), she chose tennis to get in some extra practice. Although I devoted a considerable amount of time to hitting with Chris, she did spend some time each day hitting with a few of her classmates. Because her skills were well beyond those of even the best students in the class, she rarely hit a ball into the net or out of the court. Often I would watch Chris hitting balls and at the same time giving advice to her partner. Her skills were so refined that, even when she hit with me, we could talk to each other and keep the ball in play, with only minimal attention given to the task of hitting the ball. Chris was a unconscious-competent.

Each of you started out as a unconscious-incompetent as a tennis player. This stage actually started before you had any notions about playing tennis. Just as Leigh did not know that he did not know how to walk when he was one-month old, you did not know that you did not know how to play tennis when the concept of tennis as a game was outside of your existing level of awareness. The issue we must deal here is not where you began as a tennis player because at the very least you are a conscious-incompetent. The issue we must deal with is, to what degree do you fit this profile, and what must you do to progress to the stage of conscious-competence, and further, to the stage of unconscious-competence?

There are a number of factors which affect how successfully you progress from one stage of learning to the next. And these factors at any given time may vary from student to student, and may vary in scope. In order to determine which factors had the greatest impact on a student's ability to learn new skills I found it necessary to study the learning habits of children, and in doing so discovered two qualities which stood out as the most essential elements of learning efficacy. These qualities are "curiosity" and "persistence."

You were able to walk into class today because, as an infant, you figured out a way to answer the question, *what do I need to do to walk as mommy and daddy are walking*? If at an early age you had not questioned your motor skills relative to the advanced motor skills of your parents, you may still be crawling around on hands and knees today.

Curiosity is an eagerness to know. And in the context of learning, it is an eagerness to know more about an unfamiliar aspect of your existence. When I combine this with the concept of persistence, which is the relentless pursuit of a desired goal, the question I ask is, *how can you improve a skill if you do not question why what you have is different from what you want?*

I know that as a child, this question was asked by you, just as it was asked by Leigh. One thing agreed upon by child development experts is that one of the most important tools of learning inherent in children is the quality of "imitation." A child sees something which looks interesting and exciting, and he decides that he wants to do it or have it. When Leigh observed mommy and daddy walking, walking, at some point, progressed from a non-existent entity (Leigh was an unconscious incompetent), to an unfamiliar entity which has now invaded his perceptual range of awareness, to an entity which had become interesting enough to want to imitate (Leigh was a conscious incompetent). Leigh's curiosity (why?) began the process of learning how to walk, and his persistence (desire motivation) made this goal a reality. The progression from zero knowledge to skill attainment was not possible without the knowledge (in Leigh's case implicitly expressed) that what he had was different from what he had observed.

The fact that you did not crawl to class today makes my point regarding curiosity and persistence self-evident. At some point you had to have been curious enough to ask the question, *why can't I do that*? Your being here serves as evidence that your persistence provided you with the answer. Which begs the question, how curious are you about learning the skills of tennis? The failure of many former students to learn new skills or improve their existing tennis skills was primarily the result of this question never being asked.

For years I have watched many of my students endured an endless amount of frustration on the court as they continued to produce one undesirable result after another. And the primary reason for this frustration was that these students failed to ask the question, *why? Why does the ball go left when I want it to go right? Why does the ball go into the net? Why does the ball go up too high? Why can't I hit the ball to my partner? Why does the ball get too close to me before I attempt to swing?*

Why does my forehand always hit the back fence before it bounces? These are but a few of the countless questions which are prompted by your curiosity.

In any given semester I will observe a student in my class frequently hit ball after ball virtually the same way with the same undesirable result and never (at least explicitly) question what has occurred. A student behaving in this manner, by his actions, is telling me that he is satisfied with his results. And once this state of satisfaction is reached, curiosity is inaccessible, and persistence, therefore, is exhibited only to the extent that his existing behavior is sustained.

A number of students have come to me in the past and asked for help in improving a particular stroke. Once a student named Don approached me in class with the query, "Why does the ball keep going too high on my backhand?" My response was, "Why do you think the ball keeps going too high on your backhand?" I could easily have given Don the answer he was seeking and continued on to another court to help another student with his game. I chose to respond to Don's query with one of my own because giving him the answer without challenging his existing awareness and ability to think would have only been a short-term solution. I would have solved the problem of the moment, but I am not so sure that he would have learned anything other than how to look to someone else for solutions. Before giving Don the answer, I wanted to give him a chance to exhaust the possibilities he could think of for his backhand problem. And like many students in the past, Don did find the solution. Through the process of elimination - recalling past knowledge about hitting his backhand lower, and checking this against what he was doing - Don discovered through his own initiative that he needed to adjust the angle at which his racquet met the ball on contact to match the trajectory of his swing. By questioning existing behavior, he was challenged to find the answer. And because Don embraced challenge, he was persistent enough to search until he found it.

There is no question that you are familiar with and have used the stages of learning I have just described. The individual skills and talents you possess serve as evidence that you know how to progress from a base of zero knowledge to skill development. This chapter focuses on the underlying causes of learning inefficacy which result from any attempt to circumvent the natural progression involved in learning a skill. For more than a decade I have been studying the behavior of my students, and in the process I have observed a number of skill levels and variety of problems linked to learning a new skill or improving an existing one. Close examination has shown that the problems my students experienced while attempting to learn the skills of tennis were linked to three primary causes which significantly affected their ability to progress through the stages of learning. As I discuss each cause, you may want to examine your existing behavior to see the extent to which one or more of these causes relates to any problem you may be experiencing at the moment.

The first cause is the *pathology of fear.* More than any other cause, fear may prove to be the biggest hindrance to your ability to improve your tennis skills in my class. In this section I will answer the following questions: 1) Where does fear come from?, 2) Which fears most significantly impact learning efficacy?, and 3) What can you do to overcome them? Through my own growth process I have learned that, other than the fears of loud noise and of falling we harbored as infants, *all fears harbored by adults are learned.* And, for the purpose of our discussion here, I will describe these fears as either *rational* or *irrational.*

A rational fear is one that is based upon an existing aspect of reality which *threatens your safety or well-being*. An irrational fear is a perceived aspect of reality which threatens your safety or well-being. While there are moments in your life which justify the need to be fearful, learning a skill is certainly not one of them. If you were to study children as I have for many years you will agree that the qualities of curiosity and persistence really stand out. Remember the baby crib your parents may have used to surround your playing area when you were an infant? What they failed to tell you at the time was that your crib, or playpen, was really a "cage" designed to protect you from yourself. As an infant you came into a new and exciting world. And your innate curiosity and persistence put you in a continuous and often dangerous state of exploration of your environment, within, of course, the limits of your mobility.

Your ability to crawl then walk and then run, was influenced significantly by your curiosity and persistence. The reason you often had to be protected from yourself was that your curiosity and persistence during the early stages of your development were often inconsistent with reality, or your ability to use reasoned-judgement as you explored your world. In other words, your ambition often exceeded your existing ability.

An important note here is that, as a child, when you developed certain skills and how well you developed them, depended upon striking a balance between giving full reign to your curiosity and persistence, and accepting the limits imposed on these qualities. When Leigh was an infant, my wife and I became more aware of and more in touch with current research on early childhood development. And one aspect of development which concerned us both was that of motor-skill. I attribute Leigh's ability to learn how to walk at such an early age to our decision to allow him to progress from crawling to walking naturally, without the aid of a baby walker. I have found that while convenient for parents, a baby walker often denies a child the opportunity to apply his innate abilities of curiosity and persistence to the skill of walking. Leigh fell often as he progressed (and often stumbled) through each stage of development. Yet, knowing what I know about learning efficacy, and having observed Leigh's development first-hand, a few tumbles and bruises were a small price to pay.

Let us return to the subject of improving your tennis skills. You now know that any fear you may harbor with respect to improving your tennis skills is learned. The question I ask is, *why would you fear learning*?

What I have learned from teaching hundreds of beginners is that students do not fear improvement. What they fear is *failure!* One of the most important differences I have discovered between the way children and adults approach learning is that as a rule, a child *will try until he succeeds,* whereas, an adult *will not try until he knows!* Let me explain.

At some point before Leigh was a toddler, he became aware of a more efficient mode of transportation from one end of the house to another. He was a conscious-incompetent. As his awareness expanded (watching mom and dad) so too did his curiosity, desire, and persistence. It did not matter to Leigh that learning to walk necessitated that he follow the stages of learning I have discussed. He only knew one thing, and that was that he wanted to get from here to there like mom and dad. It did not matter how often he fell, or bumped into walls. He was fearless in his pursuit. Leigh's curiosity caused him occasional pain or discomfort. Yet his desire and persistence caused him to persevere. I would say that because of his curiosity and persistence, Leigh was, in a literal sense, too unaware to be afraid of failing. Failure, in the context of learning how to walk, was not possible because Leigh could not conceptualize failure in this context. He only knew what he wanted. The notion that he should stop trying, when he did not get what he wanted on the first or second attempt, was non-existent.

I contrast this with a former student named Sarah. Sarah enrolled in my class because she expressed a desire to improve her tennis skills. She, like Leigh, was a conscious-incompetent. From the first day of class, Sarah made known her fear of stepping out on the tennis court and showing the world what she feared she could not do - hit the ball over the net. She warned me beforehand that she would be my worst student of all time and that the best teacher in the world would not be able to help her. Bear in mind that until my class, Sarah had never before been on a tennis court. Sarah had an irrational fear of failure which had been developed over time, and one which had nothing to do with the sport of tennis. Her awareness of the possibility of failure had overridden her innate curiosity and persistence. Sarah was smart enough to know - to her misfortune - that it was possible that she would not be able to hit the ball over the net.

Here you have two individuals, one, a child, the other, an adult, facing different challenges - the child learning to walk, the adult learning how to hit a tennis ball - and both starting from the same stage of learning, that of conscious-incompetence. Why are these scenarios - when played out - so vastly different? The reason a child can learn how to walk faster than an adult can learn how to hit a backhand is that the child, unlike the adult, is willing to make mistakes until he learns because he is not afraid to fail.

As an adult, the amount of success you experience in school, on the job, as an athlete, and even as a parent, will be measured by your understanding of how failure is linked to success. Regardless of who you are, the goal you attempt to achieve, or in what context, one fact remains clear: *you will never be able to eliminate the prospect of failure*. If this is true, what, then, can you do to overcome fear of failure if it is preventing you from learning?

Let us first examine how this term is used in the context of learning a skill. There are several reasons why you may fear failure. The first has to do with mistakes and the fact that you have been taught that mistakes are bad. Second, because of a personal attachment to your mistakes, you may falsely harbor the feeling that you are "bad." And because of this personal attachment, you learn to fear failure because of what failure represents - *you are a failure*! I happen to believe that the reason so many of my students have learning problems is that the fear of mistakes has caused them to embrace a definition of this term that is at best, an over-generalization, and at worst, inaccurate. I am sure you would agree that a universally accepted definition of a mistake is to *err* or *misinterpret*. From a behavioral perspective, I would say that, by this definition, when you make a mistake you are performing *out of character*. In the context of the game of tennis, it is further accepted that any time you fail in your attempt to hit the ball over the net, you have made an error. Further still, if you succeed in hitting the ball over the net, but you fail to hit a specific, pre-determined target, you again, have erred.

I have a problem with this definition, in this context. If a mistake is, to some degree, a misunderstanding, by what degree is this determined, and by whom? It is no wonder that so many students have difficulty dealing with mistakes. This term, as commonly accepted, appears to be subject to the standards of anyone who is influential enough to convince you that you have made a mistake. And when fueled by a pseudo self-concept, learning anything new becomes virtually impossible.

I prefer to use "mastery" as the standard against which a mistake should be measured. Mastery of a skill means that you have full command of the skill. And you have full command of a skill when you are operating at the limits of both your expectations and knowledge. Which tennis skill have you mastered in this class? If you have full command of your forehand stroke, then each time you hit a forehand shot into the net, or over the baseline, or hit it crosscourt when you intended to hit down-the-line, you are out of character, you have erred. If you do not have full command of your forehand stroke - you have not achieved mastery - then, by degree, I would say that it is not possible for you to perform out of character, regardless of where your forehand shot may land.

Often a student will complain to me about his backhand. He expresses incredulity at the fact that his favorite shot has hit the bottom of the net. I will ask him if his backhand has ever hit the bottom of the net before. He says "Yes." I will then ask him if, by his standard, he has mastered the backhand stroke. He says "No." I will then ask him if he feels he is performing at or near the limits of his expectations and knowledge. He says "Yes." I will then tell him that, by his own admission, he has not committed a mistake. A mistake can occur only after mastery.

In this context, you can understand my point when I say that, should you choose to hit the ball over the net or over the fence, it is not possible for me to tell you that you have committed a mistake in my class. I have taken this point to an extreme measure by offering to buy dinner for any student who hears me criticize his or a classmates's performance on court. And having taught more than two thousand students since I began this challenge, I have yet to buy a dinner.

If you can not make a mistake in my class, what happens when your shot fails to land in the proper court? In the context of learning, each time you cause an effect that is different from your intention, you have simply failed to accomplish your goal. With the negative connotation attached to the term "mistake," it is no surprise that a student will, after attending a few classes and hitting more balls into the net than into the court, decide either to drop my class or lower his aspirations to the point where a passing grade becomes his highest aim.

Failure, like curiosity and persistence, is absolutely essential to learning efficacy. And according to many experts in the field of human potential development, it is the single most important factor in the success of any high achiever, regardless of his profession or goals. As Michael Jordan says about himself, "I've failed a lot in my life, I guess that's why I succeed." Why is failure linked to success? Failure is essential to your ultimate success because it provides you with a feedback mechanism for the evaluation of completed performance. I have often heard failure referred to as the *"fertilizer of success."* Failure tells you whether or not you are true to your goal. It also reminds you that you may still have more work to do in order to achieve success. Not only is failure necessary for you to learn, it is also inevitable. I tell my students that the one way to avoid failure and to succeed is to *stop trying*! In my class, if you want to avoid failure, all you have to do is make earning a passing grade your only aim.

Failure is an immune system that provides feedback telling you something is wrong. Think about the human body. The world is full of diseases and germs which could harm you at any time. But because of your biological immune system, which requires little self-maintenance, you are able to enjoy a relatively healthy lifestyle. Pain is also a form of feedback, one that often tells you that a change in lifestyle, habit, or activity is in order. When you fail, you know that something is amiss, and that corrective action is needed.

Using failure as feedback can help you improve any aspect of your tennis performance in this class. I have demonstrated this process with many students in the past. Here is a typical scenario. As a beginning student you tell me that you want to learn how to consistently hit a forehand stroke so that you can rally with a partner across the net. Before we get to the point of implementing the steps necessary to allow you to accomplish this goal, let us review a few rudiments of the basic forehand stroke, and the laws of physics.

First, there is the grip. You must hold the racquet in such a manner that the strings will be facing the ball at impact. Second, you must stand with your left hip, shoulder, and non-racquet hand pointing in the direction of the oncoming ball (right-handed player) with your racquet pointing toward the opposite fence. Third, the starting place for your racquet-arm is at your side, in a relaxed position, with the racquet positioned so that both the handle and bottom edge are horizontal to the court. Finally, as the ball approaches, you must step toward the oncoming ball with your left foot, and time your swing so that you make contact with the ball slightly to the right of your body and before it would reach your left foot.

By now you should remember the law of cause and effect which means that the ball will land exactly where you hit it one hundred percent of the time. What, then, are the possibilities you can create with your swing? Three factors will govern where you hit any forehand. The first is racquet speed. The faster you swing, relatively speaking, the greater the distance the ball will travel. The second is the angle of the racquet when you contact the ball. Based upon the position of the racquet at contact, the ball will go to the left, right, straight ahead, up or down. The third is the trajectory of your swing. As you swing at the oncoming ball, you will either swing on an upward plane (angular momentum), or a horizontal plane (linear momentum).

Now I have just provided you with the essential elements of an "efficient" forehand stroke. Even though I have provided you with the most accurate and essential information for hitting an efficient forehand, what will ultimately determine whether or not you accomplish your goal of consistently hitting forehands to your partner will be your curiosity, persistence, and how positively you deal with failure. Suppose in your initial attempt to hit a forehand to your partner the ball goes left. What are your options? Remember you have four. One, you can hit the next shot to the correct location, which is to your partner. Two, you can stop trying and take up skiing. Three, you can hit the next forehand in the same manner and to the same location. Four, you can hit the next forehand to the right.

If you know the correct adjustment to make to hit the ball to your partner, then you will obviously choose this option because it brings you to the desired result. If you choose to stop trying and take up skiing, option two, you have allowed your fear of failure to override your curiosity and persistence, and, in essence, you have abandoned your goal. If you choose option three, hitting the next forehand to the same location as the first, you are suggesting that you have learned nothing from the first unsuccessful attempt, hence, you are bound to repeat it. If, however, you were to choose option four, hitting the next shot to a different location (to the right of your partner), you would be demonstrating that you have learned from your first failure, and even though you do not know the correct adjustment to make at this time, your curiosity and persistence will override your fear of failure and allow you to hit the ball anywhere - except to the location you know to be incorrect.

For many of my students who fear failure, this pathology is often accompanied by the fear of change. What often happens to a student suffering from this affliction is that he develops a rigid attachment to the known and familiar which overrides his innate desire to explore the unknown and unfamiliar. Through my observation of many students over the years, I have made an important discovery regarding the pathology of fear and its effect on learning efficacy. What I consistently observe in my students who fear failure is that they consider it more important to exhibit behavior that is comfortable rather than behavior that is efficacious. These students know what behavior is required to learn a particular skill, they know why it is required, and they have the capacity to exhibit this behavior. Yet, when the choice has to be made between doing what feels good at the moment and what is efficacious, more often than not, efficacy succumbs to feeling.

While the role of your emotions will be addressed in a broader context in the following chapter, I consider the effect your feelings and how you deal with change have on learning efficacy important enough to mention here as well. I can recall a number of cases where the pathology of fear, in the context of emotions, was the chief causal agent in a student's inability to improve his tennis skill.

Jackie and Tony took me literally when I explained to them that, because their grade would not depend upon where they stood on the court when they rallied, it would be acceptable if they spent the entire semester practicing within arms-length of the net. From the first day of class I observed that both Jackie and Tony were very unsure of themselves on the court. Neither had had much experience in any sports-related activity prior to taking my class. This was evident in the level of eye-hand-racquet coordination they both displayed. It took a considerable amount of effort on my part to get them comfortable with practicing on the court. I began by showing them how to rally back and forth within arms-length of the net. They both enjoyed this, and after a couple of class sessions practicing in this manner, Jackie and Tony appeared to have overcome their performance anxiety.

Because they were doing so well standing close to the net, I encouraged Jackie and Tony to think about a new challenge - moving a few steps away from the net to test their skills under new conditions. They both agreed to move further away and attempt a new challenge, and even though they managed to sustain a few modest rallies, when compared with the success experienced earlier, neither was pleased with the results. Even though Jackie and Tony had become relatively proficient with rallying from close-range, the new conditions, placing them further away from the net, brought on a new challenge that neither was ready to embrace. Each time that I would encourage them to move further away from the net, they would do so only while I stood by their court. As soon as I would leave, they would return to where they felt most comfortable. Jackie and Tony exhibited this behavior the entire semester, even though they had demonstrated on numerous occasions their ability to rally successfully from a greater distance on the court.

Stuart's problem of feelings overriding learning efficacy was reflected in his goal to develop more consistency. He confessed that he took my class to improve his consistency with his forehand

and backhand strokes. During the on-court evaluation I immediately observed why he wanted to improve his consistency. Even though he had just started playing tennis the previous summer, Stuart had developed a passion for power - he was more concerned with how hard he could hit the ball than with where he hit it. I knew, from the first day, that the key to Stuart's improvement would be a slower swing speed. For a beginning student, his technique was relatively efficient. Stuart's inconsistency was the result of his desire to hit with power overriding his awareness of the reality of the moment.

I worked with Stuart during the first few days of class, and I talked to him about reducing his swing speed so that he could sustain longer rallies with me and other students. I explained how power, control, and consistency were inextricably linked, and how hitting the ball hard was fine to the extent that he could keep it inside the lines. I used two drills with Stuart to help him reduce his swing speed. One was short-court tennis, where we rallied from close to the net and had to hit each ball on one bounce. If Stuart hit the ball too hard, it would hit the net or, if it crossed the net but did not bounce in front of me, I would catch it. For the other drill we would rally using the full court but would have to hit each ball slow enough so that it would bounce twice in the court after crossing the net.

With the use of these type of drills, Stuart's control and consistency improved almost immediately. Unfortunately Stuart did not feel comfortable with his new swing, even though he was hitting more balls over the net to his partner. The reality of the change that was occurring was surrendered to Stuart's desire to exhibit behavior that was comfortable and familiar. He would swing slow while rallying with me, however, once I left, Stuart would revert to doing what felt good rather than what was efficacious.

Even as I was in the process of creating this chapter, I became aware of still another manner in which the pathology of fear had an effect on the learning efficacy of my students in a different, although related context. My class is designed to be held outdoors. Because of the uncertainty of the weather in the fall and spring, however, I often find it necessary to conduct a number of classes in our gymnasium. Although lectures are normally the order of the day when we are indoors, consecutive days of inclement weather often necessitate the use one or more indoor sessions as an opportunity to show students how to effectively use an unconventional practice environment. In order to develop this new illustration and demonstrate the effect of the pathology of fear on learning efficacy, I must briefly allude to a concept discussed later in the text regarding emotions. Every aspect of reality that you experience is evaluated on an emotional level. In other words, you determine if an experience is beneficial to you, if it is detrimental to you, or whether it falls so low on the emotional scale it does not warrant your continuing attention.

Let us suppose that today I have decided to hold class outdoors and you have decided to attend. You would first have had to consider the emotional impact of any number of alternatives before making your choice. But having done the emotional estimate you have decided that attending is more beneficial to you than staying away. Had I decided to hold class indoors and you decided not to attend, your emotional filtering process would have been the same and not attending class would have been determined to be in your best interest; attending would not.

Examples of this decision making process are all around you and in everything you do. The inescapable conclusion that must be drawn is that the decision-making process involves placing yourself on an emotional continuum along which you move from discomfort to comfort, the preferred position being one of comfort where your fears are at their lowest.

To remove any doubt as to the relationship shared between learning efficacy and emotions, I will occasionally end class before its scheduled conclusion, especially when we are in the gym or when we are outside and it is cold. I recall the indoor session where I first discussed emotions and learning efficacy. After having students participate in a few on-court exercises for fifteen minutes to prepare them for my discussion, I lectured for another fifteen minutes and, with thirty minutes of scheduled class time remaining, took attendance and left each student with a decision to make. Having just heard my lecture on learning and emotions, and knowing that class had officially ended (at least for the purpose of earning lecture and participation points), each student would decide, by his own actions, if his highest aim that day was to learn or earn points.

The student who chose to leave after attendance had been taken did so because leaving was in his best interest while staying was not. His highest aim had been achieved when I concluded my lecture and took attendance. The student who chose to stay after attendance had been taken did so because staying was in his best interest while leaving was not. While the attendance and participation points had a level of importance, his highest aim could only be fulfilled by hitting more tennis balls, which, depending upon his effort at this point, would indicate a desire to learn.

The second cause of learning inefficacy I wish to address is the "pathology of dependence." In the context of my class, I refer to dependence as the degree to which *your capacity to learn is significantly influenced by my desire to teach.* A consistent theme throughout the book is my contention that I can not teach you anything about the game of tennis without your consent. Also true is my contention that learning efficacy, as a process, is totally dependent upon your skills of cognition and integration. It is not possible for me, or anyone else, to make you a more effective learner. Efficacy is an autonomous process, and from the day I began researching the material which defines my teaching philosophy, I have taught from the basis that, fundamentally, all knowledge or skill acquired is ***self-learned***.

During the writing of this chapter I recall working with one particular student. This happened to be the indoor session where I first discussed learning efficacy. One of the few students who remained was Marie. From the first day of class, Marie felt very uncomfortable hitting with a partner because of her limited skill, so I was not surprised by her reluctance the first time I asked her to hit a few balls with me. She appeared shocked to the point of disbelief that I would dare ask her to hit with me. In fact, her initial response to my request was, "You are too good, I can't play!" After I convinced Marie that she would be doing me a favor by allowing me to hit with her, she agreed to be my partner.

I hit with Marie for fifteen minutes, and during the entire time that we practiced, there was hardly a ball I hit to Marie that she did not manage to return. I watched Marie hit balls with a level of control, confidence, and consistency that belied her earlier categorization of her abilities. At the conclusion of our practice session, Marie remarked to me that she had never hit so many balls before in her life. I listened with interest as she continued to remark about the enjoyment she felt being able to consistently hit the ball to her partner, and how the first time she had ever hit a ball over a tennis net was when I asked her to demonstrate a drill during the first outdoor class session. She then proceeded to thank me for hitting with her and said that she was grateful that I taught her so much - which is where I stopped her.

As soon as Marie began to extol my virtues as a teacher, I found it necessary to clarify, in her mind, exactly who was responsible for her success. I told Marie that no matter how much credit she chose to give me for her success, and no matter what I thought of my skills as a teacher, I would have been totally ineffective without her *curiosity and persistence*. Marie's success during our practice session had little to do with who I was or my knowledge of tennis. Marie's success was primarily the result of *her desire to hit the tennis ball.* All I did was give her an opportunity. In fact, as I recall, during the time that we practiced together, not once did I offer any verbal instruction. Other than occasionally saying "nice job Marie," I just hit balls to her and observed her performance.

My work with learning efficacy has convinced me that all I will ever be able to do with respect to what you learn is give you information and feedback, neither of which has anything directly to do with the process by which you utilize knowledge. This explains why a student may enroll in my class and, after eight weeks, leave disappointed and with the feeling that he did not learn anything from me about the game of tennis. This type of reaction is typical of the effects of the consequence of the pathology of dependence.

The evidence I have discovered in researching this concept has convinced me that *I can not teach you efficacy.* All that I have observed as a teacher tells me that learning efficacy is not a process that is learned, *it is a process that is only forgotten*! From birth, every living entity was endowed with certain attributes which served to establish the order of the universe and the means for survival. And if you recall what I wrote in chapter one on the mind, the most important difference between you and all other living species is that you have been endowed with the ability to adjust your environment to fulfill your needs. No other living entity has this capacity, and because it was endowed at birth, no one can teach it.

What I have learned from observing my son Leigh is that, in terms of learning efficacy, the qualities of curiosity and persistence as the cornerstones of all knowledge and skill acquisition are limited only by the degree to which such pathologies as fear and dependence are reinforced. And this reinforcement begins almost from birth. What I find interesting is the fact that you started out the same as everyone else. You came into this world with no programing or instructions, only the attributes for survival. Thus, from birth, you possessed the means for learning efficacy, you simply lacked direction. Because there was no manual to guide your choices and actions at each stage of your development, your sense of efficacy was established by, and within the limits of, your mentors - parents, teachers, peers, and anyone else whose relationship with reality captured your attention.

Thus, virtually every belief you embrace in your life has some connection to beliefs of your mentors. Some of these beliefs are beneficial to your life, some of them are not. Because there is no manual to direct you towards beliefs which sustain learning efficacy or lead you away from those which suppress it, *by what means can this task be accomplished*? Logic dictates that to depend upon someone else such as a mentor to teach you efficacy means that your efficacy will again be subject to the limits of his conditioned beliefs, which are limited by his mentors' beliefs, ad infinitum. Since we are all conditioned in the same manner, it is not possible for you to reestablish your learning efficacy by depending upon the skill or knowledge of someone else. Your sense of efficacy will be reestablished to the degree that you are able to reconnect with your childhood, and to the degree that you recognize that you are, and will always be your best coach.

There is one final cause of learning inefficacy I wish to address, which, unlike fear and dependency, is not within your power of volition. It has to do with the issue of who is most directly responsible for helping you improve your tennis skills. One major difference between my class and other classes you may be taking is that here, how much and at what rate you learn will be influenced more by your classmates than by anything I do as your teacher. One essential element for learning any skill is having the opportunity to perform the skill. And in my class, your learning efficacy will be influenced by two factors: 1) The number of opportunities you have to hit tennis balls, and 2) The skill level of your practice partner. The first factor - opportunities to hit balls, is, to some degree, within your volitional control; the second factor - the skill level of your practice partner - is not.

For as long as I have been teaching the game of tennis, and with all of the knowledge I have amassed regarding teaching and learning efficacy, one aspect of the game remains resolute: *your ability to improve your tennis skills will be consistent with the number of opportunities you have to hit the ball.* Why is this important? Because for motor-skill development to occur, the number of repetitions your perform of a particular movement is key to determining how well the movement is learned. A number suggested by motor learning experts is the number two thousand. In terms of your learning, let us say, a consistent forehand motion, you would need to hit two thousand forehands before the stroke can be considered a "learned" skill. This number may not sound like much of a challenge, but let us put it into proper perspective.

To help my students understand the game from a basis of "real" numbers, I began tracking the number of tennis balls hit by a typical student over a number of class sessions. I was motivated, in part, by a study which had recently been completed assessing the playing habits of recreational tennis players. This study concluded that the average recreational player, during an hour's time on the tennis court, spent an average of ten minutes hitting tennis balls and fifty minutes doing other things (such as picking them up!). And rather than accept these findings on the basis of someone else's study, I decided to do my own research. I selected a random sampling of students from each class and tracked both the amount of time they spent hitting balls and the number of balls being hit per class over several sessions.

Interestingly, my results were very much the same as those found with recreational players. On average, a student in my class would spend ten minutes of class time hitting balls, and the remaining time doing something else. In addition, a student in my class would hit an average of one ball every four seconds, which equals fifteen balls per minute, and nine hundred balls per hour.

In the context of learning efficacy and opportunity, the numbers graphically illustrate a potential problem for you. If you are only hitting balls for ten minutes of class time, and if class meets a maximum of four times a week for eight weeks, how much learning is taking place if this is your only opportunity to hit balls? Consider that, in real numbers, we are talking about your hitting a maximum of forty-eight hundred balls during the semester, that is if you attend each class session and are able to hit balls each day you attend. Consider that my class meets in the gymnasium, on average, five times a semester, and these are usually lecture sessions which allow little time for hitting balls, and that you will probably miss a day or two for personal reasons. When you add to this the fact that the number of repetitions required for a skill to be learned applies equally to each stroke, and you have several strokes you want to improve, the potential problem with learning efficacy becomes imminently clear.

A final point I wish to make regarding opportunity, has to do with the learning environment you will be exposed to this semester. Would you take a class in macro-economics if, beforehand, you knew that the instructor knew no more or maybe less about macro-economics than you? Do you wonder why I would even ask such a question? I pose this question to you because believe it or not, in the context of improving your tennis skills, this is exactly what you are doing in my class. Remember, an essential element of learning efficacy is having a sufficient number of opportunities to repeat the skill to be learned. And guess who is primarily responsible for providing you with these opportunities? You guessed it. The person across the net, who, as a beginning student like you, *is no more likely to be qualified to teach you tennis than would be an instructor of macro-economics who had never passed basic commerce*.

Any time you attempt to learn a skill, an important factor which will significantly affect your efficacy is the degree to which your learning environment is *user friendly*. Any goal you set on any given day this semester, no matter how ambitious, will be realized to the degree that your partner performs in a manner consistent with your goal. What frequently happens in my class is that a student will tell me that he wants me to help him with his backhand. I will watch him rally with his partner only to see his partner hit each ball to his forehand side. It does not matter how much correct information I provide him. His backhand will only improve to the degree that his partner is able to direct the ball to that stroke.

Because I must devote attention to a large number of students each day, the number of opportunities you will have to hit balls with me will be limited, which means you must put your development in the hands of a classmate with the hopes that he will be able, and willing, to hit the ball to the stroke you want to improve. This is all the more reason for you to approach each class with the goal of making the most of the opportunities you will have to improve. During the first indoor session each semester I discuss the importance and advantage of the hitting wall. The wall is always there, it never misses, it always has the right attitude, and, something that can not be said about your practice partner, *it does not judge your performance*. I can not think of a better practice partner than *one who shows up every day, does not miss, and does not talk*!

As you can see, there are a number of conditions which will have an effect on your learning environment which you will not be able to control. And because of these limiting factors, bringing the right attitude to class each day is essential to your learning efficacy. This also means that it is important that you create your own opportunities by practicing outside of class time. What I have learned from former students whose tennis skills have improved over the course of a semester is that much of their success was a result of what they did away from class.

I will conclude by saying that learning efficacy begins and ends with curiosity and persistence. You began reading this chapter looking for an idea or two that would help improve your tennis skills. What you found was a reminder that your foundation for learning efficacy was in place before you enrolled in my class. You have discovered that I can not teach you what you already know and I can not give you what you already have. As a child, you were the embodiment of learning efficacy, too unaware to know that you should fear mistakes and failure, too self-assured to depend upon someone else to show you the way, and too curious and persistent to squander an opportunity to grow.

Somewhere along the way, however, you have learned to be afraid and to harbor the belief that your efficacy is in the hands of another person. I challenge you with this chapter to revisit your childhood, and to rediscover the means by which you learn to do many things well. Without question, my research into learning efficacy has convinced me that any credit you wish to give me for your success this semester must first go to you. Because the tennis skills you will develop in my class will be more a result of the efficacy you have brought to the court than what you may claim to have learned from me.

Chapter 9
Emotions, Pressure and Stress

In chapter one I mentioned that a number of former students enrolled in my class with the mistaken belief that the primary tool they would need to achieve their goals would be their tennis racquet. These students examined the course content, credit, and structure, and decided that success could be achieved without engaging their ability to think efficiently. This would explain how a large number of my students either failed to improve their tennis skills, or failed to earn the grade they desired, or both. In addition to the number of former students who failed to realize their desired goal, an equal number of former students either dropped my class, or, turned what should have been a "no brainer" into a class where the anxiety and stress experienced reached a level which far exceeded the demands of the class.

In searching for reasons as to why an elective activity class should cause such misery for students who, by all accounts, have demonstrated their ability to handle course work far more demanding than anything I could possibly offer in an introductory tennis class, I found that, without question, the underlying pathology for students experiencing difficulty with my class was the manner in which they engaged the process of thinking. It is because of this that I found it necessary to devote an entire chapter to the mind, and it is also the reason that I would like to discuss how your method of thinking relates to your "*Emotions*," and thus, your ability to manage "*Stress*."

Every aspect of reality which enters your perceptual range of awareness in this class will be classified as either beneficial to you, harmful to you, or not important enough to warrant any further attention. You may be hitting balls on court three and notice a classmate hitting balls on an adjacent court. He is within your perceptual range of awareness but his existence has no relevance to you at the moment. His being on an adjacent court is neither beneficial nor harmful to you. Contrast this with your partner across the net. If you are just practicing, with no score being kept, and he is hitting the ball to you in a manner which allows you to work on your performance goals, he too is within your perceptual range of awareness and this experience would probably be considered beneficial. If, however, you were practicing, and your partner chose to hit balls in a manner that made it difficult for you to work on your performance goals, he is also within your perceptual range of awareness, however, this experience would probably be considered harmful.

Over the course of this semester, you will undoubtedly be exposed to a number of experiences which you will assess in some manner as being either beneficial or harmful. This is the role of your emotions. An emotion is *a psychosomatic estimate of the relationship between any perceived aspect of reality and yourself.* This feeling component of the mind will allow you to decide, instantaneously, which actions will be beneficial to you this semester and which will be harmful. The problem with emotions is that there is no apparent connection between what you feel to be beneficial or harmful, and what is, in reality, beneficial or harmful. It is this lack of congruity between your feelings and reality that this chapter will address. The ideas I will present are designed to add clarity to your understanding of how emotions and stress will affect your goal achievement.

I will begin by stating that from the first day I presented this course to my students and observed the difficulty some had in achieving their goals, I never questioned their cognitive skills. Any student who is in a position to enroll in my class would only be in this position by virtue of a track record of demonstrated cognitive efficacy. What I have questioned, however, is the manner in which some students have engaged this process in the context of succeeding in my class. What I have found is that the student who experiences difficulty with my class tends to be one who uses *emotion as a tool of cognition*, and whose actions are based more upon *what feels right than upon what is right in terms of reality*. The following examples illustrate this point.

Jim knew, as did each of my students, that the only way he was going to improve his tennis skills was to attend class and practice with a specific purpose. Even though he stated that he wanted to learn how to hit a topspin backhand, Jim did not embrace the prospect of having to use his practice time to change his stroke pattern. Because he enjoyed playing tennis and this was his only opportunity to play during the semester, Jim's desire to want to change, and possibly improve his backhand, always yielded to his desire to hit an underspin backhand, which is what felt good.

Sharon, who indicated early on that she needed an "A" to get off of academic probation, was aware of my grading policy at the start of the semester. She knew that even though learning was not necessarily required to pass, she still needed to attend class and participate with regularity. She was also aware that lecture days provided an opportunity to earn a significant number of points toward her grade without having to hit any tennis balls. Even in the presence of such a liberal grading policy, Sharon found a way to struggle through the semester, missing the first three lectures and numerous outdoor classes. It did not seem to matter to Sharon that each missed class was putting her desired grade in jeopardy. Apparently she was content with attending class only when she felt like attending.

Frank's problem was that he had a disdain for hitting tennis balls on a gymnasium floor or against a wall. One particular semester we had an unfortunate stretch of inclement weather which forced us to spend a considerable number of classes in the gym. Because Frank enrolled in my class with the idea that he would be able to practice his serve and play games, he rarely attended class when we could not practice outside. As a result, because of attendance problems, Frank was forced to choose between a *"C"* and an *"Incomplete."*

Pete and Joann's problems had little to do with skill development or with hitting balls in the gym. It turned out that they enrolled in the class so that they could practice and spend some social time together. While the semester started out fine for both Pete and Joann with respect to attendance, I could not help but notice that as Pete's attendance became irregular, so did Joann's. Even though they both wanted to learn the skills of tennis, and they both needed to pass my class, one never attended class without the other. In fact, on a number of occasions, Joann arrived early, anticipating that Pete would arrive later. Once she discovered that Pete was not going to show, she felt it more important to find Pete than to participate and earn points toward her grade.

Each student just mentioned had the same real, underlying problem which was using emotion as a tool of cognition. Each chose to act in a manner consistent with what he felt appropriate even though this course of action was inconsistent with his stated goal. I do not know your goals this semester. You may be here to learn how to play tennis. You may be here to earn a grade. You may be here to earn course credit to maintain your academic status. Regardless of your reason for being here, your success will be determined by the manner in which you engage the process of thinking. And for you to succeed in my class, your thinking must emanate from a basis of *reasoned-judgement.*

What is reason? *Reason is the human faculty which identifies and integrates evidence provided by the senses.* Reasoned-judgement therefore, is the process of choosing a course of action based upon what you perceive to be right, and right in this context is that which is consistent with reality. What then is reality? *Reality is any evidence provided by the senses which can be considered axiomatic, or self-evident*, the most fundamental examples of this concept being existence, consciousness, and identity.

If the faculty of reason identifies reality - that "A" is "A," then it is the faculty of emotion (feelings) which evaluates each aspect of reality that enters your range of perceptual awareness, and thus determines which aspects of reality are beneficial or harmful to you according to your values. A point I have stressed in my class from the beginning is that reality is not capricious. Reality does not change because your feelings change. Regardless of how you choose to evaluate any evidence of reality provided by your senses, what will remain consistent for each of you is that fact that what is, is.

In the context of this class and your goals, each of you must accept the reality that in order for you to earn a passing grade, certain requirements must be met. Having seen many students fail to earn their desired grade in a class where intellectual aptitude is not necessarily a requisite, I am convinced that too often students replace reason with emotion as a tool of cognition. There are two specific reasons for this pathology, one related to past conditioning, the other related to the nature and structure of this class with respect to your values.

After observing, even in myself, the widespread use of emotions as a means of knowing reality, and knowing the struggle many students have had with a tennis class requiring minimal intellectual aptitude, I am led to believe that the use of reason as a means of knowing reality, and the use of reasoned-judgement as the guide for one's choices and actions, is not an innate skill. It must be learned. If this is true, then ask yourself, *how much training, formal or otherwise, have I had in reality-based thinking*? (Again, taking myself as an example, I know that I have encountered many situations which required that I proceed with reason rather than emotion. Yet I do not recall being trained in the judicious use of reason versus emotion either by my parents or through formal education. Inevitably, I would find out whether my actions were guided by reason or by emotion through the consequences of my behavior relative to my environment. In other words, most of my insight into the connection between emotions and thinking efficacy has come through trial and error. I began studying reason as a tool of cognition on my own, long after my formal education had ended. And even now, as I write about emotions, because of past conditioning, I still find myself in the *conscious-competent* stage of learning with respect to using reason instead of emotion as my primary tool of cognition.)

Past conditioning will have a lot to do with your success in this class. With reason as your tool of cognition, nothing in this class will challenge you beyond the limits of your capacity to find a way to achieve your goal. If a passing grade is your highest aim, I will not have to remind you that attendance and participation are the requirements you must meet to realize your goal. You will recognize the truth about reality. And you will know that this reality will only be accomplished through the pursuit of a course of action consistent with your stated goal. If learning more about the game of tennis is your highest aim, I will not have to remind you that improvement comes as the result of purposeful practice. You will know that learning the skills of tennis is a challenge which will require you to face the prospect of failure as you attempt to progress through the stages of learning with each new skill. You will know that your practice partner may or may not have similar skills or performance goals, and that each class session and practice experience is to be viewed as an opportunity to focus on achieving goals and overcoming obstacles, not a time for indulging distractions.

On the other hand, should you choose to use emotion as a tool of cognition, you will be challenged by any number of conditions in my class. When you feel it is too hot or cold outside to suit your needs, you may not feel like attending class, even though you need the practice and the points toward your grade. When you attend class outside and can not find the ideal practice partner, you may not feel like hitting balls, or, you may do so reluctantly out of a sense of obligation to earn points toward your grade, rather than because you want to improve your skills. When class is held in the gym, and you do not feel like listening to a lecture or hitting balls on a gym floor, it will be easy for you to forget about the virtues to be found in this practice environment, or, more importantly, the significant number of points available toward your grade if I lecture.

Apart from the manner in which you have been conditioned, I have found that the nature and structure of my class significantly affects the extent to which you may use emotion or reason as your primary tool of cognition. Because tennis is a game, your decision to enroll in my class was based, in part, on your desire to engage in a fun, recreational activity, not an intellectual pursuit designed to challenge and improve your cognitive efficacy. By structuring the class in a manner which allows you to pursue the game on your own terms - you may learn as much or little as you like - and also choose how you wish to be graded, I have, in essence, removed any external incentive for you to bring the tool of reason to the tennis court. If this were chemistry or philosophy or engineering, the need for the tool of reason would be self-evident, and expected. In my class, however, while the need for the tool of reason is also self-evident, unlike chemistry, philosophy, or engineering, it is not necessarily expected. What has happened to many former students is that the need for reasoned-judgement was often discovered at or near the end of the semester, at which time they were forced to resort to extreme measures to earn a passing grade. Unfortunately, for some, this discovery was made too late. And aside from the grade, failure to make this discovery early in the semester affected the extent to which they were able to realize their performance goals.

The need for reason as a tool of cognition in my class will be the same for the student whose highest aim is to achieve a passing grade and the student whose highest aim is that of learning how to hit a better forehand. You must be careful not to let the nature and structure of my class lead to you believe that you can earn a passing grade or improve your tennis skills through any means other than exercising to the fullest, your capacity to think.

I would now like to turn your attention to the pathology of emotion as a tool of cognition in a different context, which is your ability to manage pressure and stress. From the first semester that I taught a college tennis course, I felt a need to address the concepts of pressure and stress. As a coach I already knew how these conditions affected the performance of the competitive athlete. And as soon as I began teaching tennis to college students, I quickly realized that even in the absence of competition, the effect of these factors on my students was too significant to dismiss. My desire to include a discussion on pressure and stress in an introductory tennis class was fueled further by a seminar I attended in May of 1984. The invited speaker at this seminar was well-known sport psychologist Dr. Robert Kriegel, who, as a competitive swimmer, barely missed earning a spot on the United States Olympic Swim Team in 1972. His presentation on stress was part of a series of seminars being held on college campuses throughout the United States.

The seminar was a presentation of the results of a year-long study on the effects of pressure and stress on selected individuals in the United States. Participants in the study came from a variety of backgrounds, and what was shared by each was an acute predisposition for stress as a pathological condition due to the nature of their occupation or predominant daily activity. What was interesting about the findings of this study was that, of all the groups studied, the one in which the negative effect of stress was the most acute was college students. This in spite of the fact that the study included firemen, policemen, window washers, surgeons, race car drivers, parents, and jet pilots. What was discovered during the study was that few life experiences can match the pressure-cooker environment college students are forced to endure in their pursuit of knowledge and, ultimately, a chosen career.

While a number of factors may contribute to this condition, the two I am most concerned with are *control* and *pressure*. In chapter one I talked about how important having a sense of control over your life is to your psychological and emotional well-being. What was discovered during this study was that, in a perceptual or psychosomatic sense, the locus of control you at one time experienced within, has shifted in the college environment because of personal expectations and the expectations of other people. Let us look at two very familiar scenarios.

In scenario one you are taking a full course load for the semester, and, as far as each of your instructors is concerned, you have no outside life. You are a full-time student taking one class - *his*! But you also work, performing daily tasks which are totally unrelated to your career aspirations, and you are employed by a boss whose work is his life and who therefore, expects from you, unyielding devotion to the job.

Scenario two places you at home living with your parents or a spouse. Apart from the expectations placed on you regarding family issues, living at home means you commute to school and are subject to the uncertainties of public transportation or traffic congestion on the highway, or a temperamental car that seems to have a mind of its own and starts when it wants to. And all of this to get to a class where the instructor grades on attendance and is unaware of or unconcerned that you travel a considerable distance to get to school.

These and other circumstances simply add to the number of factors which facilitate this perceived loss of control, and this condition is exacerbated by the limits of time. Think about how often you have enrolled in a class where the instructor has given you twenty weeks of assigned work to complete in sixteen. And keep in mind, you must endure these pressures for four or more years with no guarantee of gainful employment when it is over, nor even of a job related to your major.

These external demands must be managed daily, and when compounded with your own expectations, which are often inconsistent with the expectations of others, the natural result is tension. The degree of tension you experience is directly related to the degree to which perceived external pressure is inconsistent with personal expectations. And the manner in which you relieve this tension determines the degree to which the stress you experience is *helpful* or *harmful.*

Prior to attending this seminar, my interest in stress had been limited to its relationship to competitive performance. As a coach I knew that stress was a factor which needed to be addressed if I was going to help my team members improve their competitive skills. It was only after this seminar that I began to apply my knowledge in this area to teaching beginning tennis students. And without question, my work in this area has influenced my approach to teaching more than any other single concept.

What is stress? *Stress is your response to perceived physical or psychological change or threat.* Pressure is a psychosomatic interpretation of change or threat, and tension is an internal state created by the degree to which this interpretation deviates from your desired physical or psychological comfort. And your emotions determine the degree to which any change is important to your life relative to your values. Are pressure and stress beneficial or harmful? The answer is both. They can be beneficial or harmful, depending upon how you choose to deal with change. Your emotions determine whether or not change or threat is to be valued. Pressure is experienced to the degree that change or threat is valued. The degree of tension you experience is measured by the degree to which you leave your comfort zone. And this deviation determines the degree to which your stress response is positive or negative.

Because of what I have learned about stress subsequent to attending this seminar, I am convinced, more than ever, that the worst thing I could possible do to you in my class is harbor the expectation that you should be here primarily to learn more about the game of tennis and improve your on-court skills. As you read further, you will discover that nothing would be more inimical to your life this semester than for your grade to be determined by your on-court performance.

To understand why I would adopt a teaching philosophy which, by all accounts, appears to be the antithesis of what I have been trained to do as an educator, I must state my purpose with you this semester from the broadest possible context, which is, *how can I help you regain or sustain your sense of autonomy*? Everything I attempt to do this semester must answer to this question, from the on-court activity to the lectures and practice sessions in the gym. I have found that any effort on my part to promote autonomy begins and ends with the manner in which you handle your life when the ball does not bounce your way.

It would not surprise me were you to view with incredulity, my decision to write a book for a tennis class that not only fails to address proper tennis technique or how to keep score in a match, but one that challenges the notion that learning more about the game and improving your tennis skills should be your highest virtue as a student. Until I began studying the effect of stress on college students, the notion of learning more about the game of tennis was, by all accounts, my only virtue as a teacher. It was only subsequent to my decision to view you, my student, as a total person, that I realized so much more could be accomplished during our short time together if I would dare to look beyond the lines for answers to your problems. And here is what I have learned.

Stress is a *self-creation*. Any stress you encounter from birth to death is already inside of you. This also tells me that there is absolutely no stress in the environment. Stress does not come from school, from work, from family, or friends, and it certainly does not come from the game of tennis or my class. I know that stress is a response to pressure, and that pressure is the degree to which perceived external expectations differ from your own. And I know that your emotions determine which aspects of reality you value, which in turn, determines when and where you are likely to perceive pressure.

Further, looking at the nature of higher education, I have found a preponderance of evidence which suggests that the two most important functions of the system you must pass through in pursuit of your chosen career are that of teaching you how to think critically, and how to use this skill to successfully deal with both the challenges of your career and of life. That an institution of higher education would hold thinking and challenge as virtuous is not the problem. The problem I wish to address is that of *balance*.

I have found that with all its virtues, the problem with higher education is that your entire life takes on a state of perpetual motion, where each day you must deal with an on-going series of demands, expectations, and deadlines, with each professor concerned about you only to the extent that you fulfill the requirements of his class. How often, for example, have you had a professor ask you if you could use a little more time to turn in an assignment, or if he should change an examination date because you have a date in traffic court because someone hit your car while it was parked on the street, because in order to get to his class on time you could not park in your lot across campus? How often has a professor given you a day off from his class just for the purpose of allowing you time to either study for an examination in another class or to allow you to get an early start on your thirty-mile commute home? How about a professor having a class session where the assignment of the day is a group discussion about your life, and how you and fellow classmates are dealing with challenges of school and outside activities? When was the last time you had a lecture or discussion class where the assignment of the day was a leisure stroll or jog around campus?

You may wonder, *what does this any of this have to do with the mission of higher education*? In my opinion, *everything*.

If stress can only be released, and if stress is a response to the tension created by the pressure of internal and external expectations, and if pressure is the centerpiece of your life as a college student, the question is not whether or not stress has to be released. The question is *how*?

Throughout man's evolution, many advances have been made in the field of mental health, yet, today, aside from medication, there still exists only two methods for you to relieve the tension brought on by pressure: *exercise and behavior modification*. The importance of each method will be addressed later, but I would like to first explain why they work.

Exercise provides both physical and psychological benefit in that physical fitness *boost self-confidence* and facilitates autonomy. You not only feel better about yourself, *but you also feel more in control* - a key factor which determines whether or not the stress you experience is positive. Exercise is the most readily accessible activity in which you control the *duration*, *intensity,* and *frequency* of activity. You can go for a walk, jog, swim, ride a bike, play tennis, or engage in any other form of activity which involves the aerobic system. What is key is that whatever activity you choose, you participate at a level that is comfortable and one that does not add to or sustain the very tension you are seeking to relieve.

The beneficial effect of exercise with respect to your cognitive efficacy has been substantiated in a Harvard University Study. This study involved two groups of students. In one group, students were asked to spend all of their available time prior to examinations studying course material. In the other, students were asked to maintain their normal study habits, but with one change. Each student was asked to use his spare time engaging in a form of physical activity of his choosing. When examination grades were compared, the group which studied less and exercised, performed better than the group which did nothing but study course material. The conclusion of the study was that, all other factors being equal, the student who supplements normal study habits with exercise, will probably perform better at examination time than the student who devotes all of his time to mentally "cramming."

Exercise done in moderation is invaluable as a tension reducing activity. And speaking from experience, the more relaxed you are going into a pressure situation, such as a final exam, the more likely you are to be at your cognitive best.

As for behavior modification, no greater tool exists for your mental health and cognitive efficacy than your ability to adjust your attitude or outlook with respect to conditions in your life you can not control. The right attitude will not change an aspect of reality you must face that is undesirable; it just makes this undesirable aspect of reality less threatening, emotionally. As a college student, you must face the reality of examinations, a condition you can not control. Your control over the outcome of your performance on examinations is limited by your cognitive efficacy - which is not self-evident nor automatic - and your ability to have the right attitude relative to the desired outcome. The pressure you perceive and tension you experience when faced with an examination are relative to your expectations. *Do you expect to pass or fail*? If you expect to pass, it is to this degree that you will embrace pressure and experience minimal tension. If you expect to fail, it is to this degree that you will fear pressure and experience undue tension.

While other factors affect performance on examinations, such as preparation and difficulty of subject matter, it is clear that these conditions aside, the attitude you choose to adopt will significantly affect the degree and type of stress you experience.

The importance of exercise and attitude are better understood when viewed in the context of your life as a college student. The demands and expectations that impact your life remain relatively constant for each of you in my class. The ones which are most consistent are rather obvious - classes and required assignments, finances, relationships, and time. So too are the ones which are less consistent - career choice, cognitive aptitude, self-confidence, self-concept, emotions, and values. What is not so obvious is the relationship between the demands and expectations you must face which are external, and those which are internal, and the pressure created when the two are not in harmony.

I said college is a pressure cooker environment where, from start to finish, you are exposed to a perpetual cycle of demands and expectations from professors, any one of whom often has only one concern: *getting through the curriculum in any given semester regardless of how much work this imposes on his students*. Not that this is not enough to wreak havoc with your ability to deal with stress, but you must still add to this, the demands and expectations of friends and family, your boss at work, and other time constraints. All of this is pressure, which is external. And internally, you must now confront your own demands and expectations, which are related to your *self-efficacy* - cognitive aptitude, self-confidence, self-concept, emotions, and values.

What you are faced with, therefore, is a cycle of demands and expectations, both internal and external, all of which create pressure and thus, tension. My question is, *where is the relief*? If stress is the result of relieving the tension brought on by pressure, and if this process is the natural consequence and necessary function of being human, what pressure relieving opportunities are you provided as a student?

The most difficult challenge facing higher education today is that of creating balance between the pressure you must face in your pursuit of knowledge and the relief necessary for you to reach and sustain the highest level of cognitive efficacy. I am the first to admit that college students need to learn how to effectively manage pressure. I would take a dim view of facing open-heart surgery knowing that my doctor, in pursuit of his medical degree, took every class *pass/fail*! With my life on the line, I want to know that my operation is not his first encounter with pressure. But I also contend that when a student is subjected to constant pressure and not provided with adequate relief, the end result is not always in his best interest.

As a college student, you face one of two scenarios. If your internal and external expectations are relatively consistent, you will embrace the pressure of pursuing a college degree, and success will be your reward. If, however, these expectations are inconsistent and remain so, you will eventually succumb to the pressure of pursuing a college degree and success will elude you. You will leave college or be dropped. The reality of your life as a student is clear. You know that once you begin, you will leave college in one of two ways: *with a degree or without*. And this knowledge in itself creates a level of pressure too stressful for some individuals; the notion of attending college is never entertained.

This brings us to my teaching philosophy. Because of what I know about your life beyond my class - the pressures, demands and expectations, both self-imposed and imposed by others - and the respite from these conditions you seldom enjoy, I see little value to be gained from my class becoming one more condition in your life that, potentially, will be perceived as an emotional threat. And because I know that you have more conditions in your life which are pressure inducing rather than pressure relieving, I see that the greatest gift I can give to you, as a condition in your life, is an opportunity to experience balance.

How have I done this? First, by giving you *an opportunity to exercise in a non-threatening environment*. Because your grade in my class is not necessarily performance-based, you are free to attend class and hit balls without the pressure of having to hit a specified number of balls to a specified target. You are also free to learn and improve at a pace according to your own agenda, not the agenda of other classmates, nor one set by me. I know that if exercise is to help you relieve stress, you must control the intensity, duration, and frequency. Even when class is held indoors on the gym floor, and all you have at your disposal is the wall, hitting balls under these conditions could prove more beneficial in terms of balance than skipping class because you do not have a court, a net, and a practice partner. This sense of balance and control will not be possible if the threat of a failing grade becomes your primary motivation for attending class.

Second, each chapter in this book, and the accompanying lectures, provide you with an opportunity to read about, listen to, and integrate ideas which will help you adjust your attitude to match the conditions in your life at any given moment. The reading material is connected to your grade only to the extent that you are required to explain, in your words, the relationship between what I have written and what you may experience during the semester. Your written assignments are not graded on how consistent your view of reality is with my own. You are graded and rewarded for introspection, for saying what you feel about you. Because of this, you can not fail this assignment, and, therefore, the only expectations you must fulfill are your own.

My greatest challenge this semester will be that of providing you with evidence to support my contention that the stress benefits derived from exercise and behavior modification can only be experienced in my class to the extent that you are free to participate without your grade hanging in the balance, and that the decision to learn new, or improve existing tennis skills, must rest with you. While the evidence is there, it may not be enough to overcome your belief that you will only learn or improve if your grade hangs in the balance, or, by living up to my expectations rather than your own. I will say that as an individual, you may be the one student who has enough balance to handle the pressure of your grade resting with skill acquisition, and you may readily embrace the idea of an "outcome-based" approach to an introductory tennis class. I do not discount the fact that you and other students may have the expectations, time, commitment, and the attitude to live up to the challenge of learning new, or improving existing tennis skills. Experience has shown, however, that the number of former students who have complained to me about not being graded on performance has been far outweighed by the number of students who welcomed the opportunity to learn and improve as a matter of choice, and not as the means to which a passing grade is the end.

Finally, there is another reason I offer you the opportunity to learn more about the game of tennis in a non-threatening environment, a reason less related to the issue of stress and more related to the game itself. I am a firm believer in the adage that *you only have one chance to make a first impression.* This is just as true of the game of tennis as it is of people. If this is your first exposure to learning how to play tennis, the opinion formed by your experience this semester will last a lifetime. It will only take a few class sessions for you to decide whether or not the game is fun, and this decision will probably be based upon how often you are able to hit the ball over the net and between the lines. The problem is not that the game is difficult. The problem is that of time. Tennis Tennis skills are not developed overnight. This activity requires a time commitment relative to the level of performance you seek, and this time commitment is no different than that of any class you may be taking where your goal is to learn something of value. Unless you are embarking on a professional tennis career, in all likelihood, you will not have an abundance of time to devote to your tennis development beyond the limits of my class. Time constraints, when combined with the inherent challenge of learning a skill and fulfilling expectations - both yours and mine - could potentially become threatening (emotionally) to the extent that any pressure and tension you experience negates the enjoyment which you, at one time, desired.

I have chosen a carte blanche approach to my class even with the knowledge that giving you absolute freedom to choose the extent to which you will approach the game of tennis is not a panacea; you may, for reasons unrelated to my class structure or philosophy, still find the challenge of learning more about the game more than you can handle at this time in your life. Unquestionably, the evidence is overwhelming which suggests that my teaching approach serves the needs of the majority of my students, and I can not, in good conscience, deny it. Further, I realize too, that such an approach to teaching may prove overwhelming to you, intellectually and conceptually, as it rubs against the grain of traditional educational theory, and its "leverage" mentality. When the course philosophy is viewed in an emotional-perceptual context (feelings as a means of knowing reality), any degree of discomfort you experience will be understood. When, however, it is viewed in a conceptual-perceptual context (reasoned-judgement as a means of knowing reality), this non-threatening introduction to the game could prove to be therapeutic, both psychologically and emotionally.

I hope this chapter has added clarity to your understanding of how emotions, pressure, and stress relate to your success in my class and to the manner in which this class is taught. If it has done nothing more than ease, for one day, the tension you may experience as a student, then, regardless of the degree to which you have learned something about the game of tennis, it has adequately served its purpose.

Chapter 10

Mental Health

The decision to include a chapter on mental health in this book was not an idea I entertained until the final weeks of my writing. I have, after all, devoted a considerable amount of textual material to ideas not commonly found in a book created for a college tennis course, and until this time, I felt that my purpose of addressing pathologies related to the mind had been adequately served. However, during the final weeks of preparing the manuscript, I decided that I would include a brief discussion of the four attributes of mental health which, while related to other parts of the book, were equally deserving of attention on their own.

This chapter will serve a dual purpose. If you have read the book from the beginning, you probably understand, quite well, the philosophy I espouse. For you, this chapter will serve as a summary. If, for some reason, you have chosen this point to begin your reading, then this chapter will, hopefully, encourage you to read further.

I will begin by stating that while ***Tennis for Everyone*** has been written for my college introductory tennis course, this book, and its philosophy, is not about *tennis*. I have written about common problems you face, every day, on the tennis court, but these problems reach beyond the boundaries of the game. I have written about uncommon solutions to these problems, solutions which are meant, ultimately, to move you toward autonomy, heightened awareness of self, and personal fulfillment. I have written about the game of tennis and the game of life, and how the vicissitudes experienced in both arenas are inextricably linked. The principles which guide your movement toward a better backhand are the same ones which guide your movement toward earning a college degree. How you handle success or failure in one arena is a reflection of how it will be handled in the other.

To bring a sense of closure to this book, and the class for which it is written, I would like to discuss mental health as the "holy grail" to which each of you would like to ascend, and the attributes which define this state, and which are essential to its attainment. The first is the quality of *happiness*. As one of man's highest aims, much of what you experience in life will in some way be linked to the degree to which you enjoy the direction in which your life is moving. Nothing will be pursued by you with more intensity than experiences which will bring pleasure to your existence. This is quite evident in the behavior of the student who, on occasion, chooses a course of action in my class that is beneficial to his life in an emotional context, even though, in the context of reality, it is inimical to his grade. Such will be the case of the student who does his last minute studying for a test in another class while in attendance in my class. This is also quite evident in the behavior of the employee who, because he feels underpaid, considers himself entitled to steal from his employer. The illegally gained income is beneficial on an emotional level yet it is inimical to his sense of ethics and loyalty to his company.

Your capacity to experience happiness is innate and endowed at birth. The question, therefore, is not, *should happiness be viewed as virtuous?*, but *how is it to be experienced in the context of mental health?* Two principles which make happiness and mental health symbiotic are "morality" and "reason." Morality tells you that your right to experience happiness ends with another person's right to do the same. A person authentic to this principle understands that when he is employed by a company, he can not decide, because of an emotional "urge," that he is entitled to company funds that are not earned. Reason tells you that your right to experience happiness ends with the dictates of logic, and the extent to which fulfilling an emotional urge will, in the end, prove inimical to this experience. The student authentic to this principle understands that when he enrolls in this class, he can not attempt to violate the course requirements with impunity, because of an emotional need to avoid hearing a lecture or practicing on a gym floor.

The second attribute is the quality of *perspective*. Perspective, in the context of mental health, is *the degree to which your interpretation of the world is consistent with reality*. Your perspective is narrow to the degree that you view reality with an emotional-perceptual consciousness. It is broad to the degree that you view reality through the eye of reason.

You are driving home from school one day, and while on the highway, a car speeds by and cuts you off, causing no threat to your immediate safety, but forcing you to suddenly swerve and hit your brakes. A narrow perspective (emotion as your tool of thought) will cause you to react in anger and speed up in retaliation. After all, how dare someone invade your space on the highway? A broad perspective (reason as your tool of thought) will cause you to think about the possible reason this individual is choosing to act in such an inconsiderate and potentially dangerous manner. Reason would tell you that it is possible that this individual has just received a call about a possible heart attack at home and *he is rushing home to be of service*.

As a student you enrolled in my class with the expectation that you would be hitting tennis balls on a real court with a practice partner possessing similar skill. You then discover that you are the only student who can consistently hit three balls over the net, and because of unseasonable weather, much of your class time is spent in the gym listening to lectures and hitting balls against a wall. A narrow perspective will cause you to stop attending class when the conditions do not suit your emotional needs, and when you do attend, you will pick only the best practice partner available or practice serves when class is held outside. When class is indoors, you will reluctantly make a feeble attempt to practice against the wall, and my lectures will be used as an opportunity to catch up on homework from another class or the sleep you were deprived of the night before. A broad perspective will cause you to evaluate the conditions you can not change in a class you enrolled in by choice. You will practice with any classmate who is available, recognizing that even with a partner not blessed with similar skill can help you improve. And personal gain aside, you will see this as an opportunity to help a fellow classmate, much the same as someone in your past helped you. When class is held indoors, the hitting wall will be embraced as a chance to work on your strokes in a more controlled environment than one in which the elements which affect performance are many, and much less predictable. And lectures will be viewed as an opportunity to gain insight, into yourself and the game. You will appreciate the fact that you have a chance to learn something about life with "no strings attached" because you will be free to listen to and accept ideas which are beneficial and reject those which are not.

The third attribute is the principle of *freedom*. Probably the most important element of mental health, freedom means that *you have options*. Regardless of the complexity or simplicity of your life pursuits, the degree to which you enjoy mental health, and thus, personal fulfillment, will be measured first by *the options you see*, and second, by *the options you choose*.

How much freedom do you have as a student? More specifically, *how much freedom do you perceive*? To understand the magnitude to which this principle impedes or promotes mental health, I offer the following exchange between student and instructor, one which has taken place in my class on more than one occasion. "Professor, I am sorry but I can not attend class today." "Why?" "Because I have to study for an economics examination, which happens to be my major." "Well, you know that I can not give you credit for attendance if you leave before the end of class. And as you know, you are falling behind in points, something which potentially will lower your grade." "But I need an "A" in order to graduate Professor, so how can I make up my points?" "You can make up points by attending my afternoon class which meets on Mondays and Wednesdays." "But I can not do that because I have to work Monday and I have a biology lab Wednesday afternoon and if I do not complete my project, I am afraid I might fail the course." "Well there is one more tennis match you can attend for extra credit that will be played tomorrow at three o'clock." "But tomorrow I have a meeting with my college advisor about graduate school which was scheduled two weeks ago!"

If these were conditions in your life right now, it would be easy for you to feel a sense of imprisonment brought on by the apparent lack of options seen in this scenario. It seems that this student is wedged between the proverbial "rock and a hard place," being forced to choose from a limited number of options, none of which appear to lead to a desirable outcome, an "A" in tennis. This perception is the pathology of a narrow perspective. His feeling of imprisonment was not caused by a lack of options. It was caused by his refusal to choose from among the options he, by his own admission, possessed. One option was that he could attend class on the day in question. Even though it meant giving up study time for an examination, which might result in an undesirable grade in this class, it was still an option. Another option was to go to tennis class but elect to study for the economics examination rather than participate. Because points can still be earned for attendance, both goals would, to some extent, be realized. Attending class on Monday was another option he could have exercised. He could have taken the day off, left early, or arrived late. Skipping the biology lab was another option he could have chosen. How about the meeting with the college advisor? He could have missed this meeting altogether, or, called and canceled, or asked for a new appointment, stating a family emergency as the reason. Again, these are all options.

The truth is, options such the ones identified above are often overlooked because they do not allow you to *have your cake and eat it too*. Options are not always pleasant, or enjoyable, or what we would want if the situation were different, but they are always there. I am reminded of the story told of Jack Benny, a comedian well know for his penchant for holding on to money. He allegedly was once approached by a robber who repeatedly asked of Mr. Benny, "Your money or your life, your money or your life," to which Jack replied (after a long pause), "I'm thinking, I'm thinking!" You see, even under the most extraordinary circumstances, you still have options!

What I have learned from studying people is that the problem with enjoying mental health is not the absence of options. *Options are always there*. The problem is that you may not want to accept the often *undesirable consequences* which may accompany these options. The student depicted above is not afraid of his options. He is afraid of the consequences which accompany each option. The choice of giving up study time for economics is not the problem; the consequence of an *undesirable grade* is. The choice of skipping biology is not the problem; the consequence of a *failing grade* is. The choice of missing work is not the problem; the consequence of *losing income or a job* is. The choice of missing the meeting with the college advisor is not the problem; the consequence of *not being admitted to graduate school* is.

When I say that <u>everything in life is an option</u>, I mean this quite literally. From the cradle to the grave, the range of your options in life increase relative to your range of awareness. The problem is that every option carries a consequence, and these consequences are not always desirable. Thus, in order for you to enjoy the freedom of choice, as a component of mental health, you must understand, and accept the fourth attribute which is the principle of *responsibility.*

This is where most of my students, like most people in life, have the greatest difficulty. Accepting responsibility is the most important attribute of mental health, and without it, you will be incapable of fully experiencing the attributes of happiness, freedom, and perspective. And the behavior of students in my class over the years has proven to me that in order for responsibility to be learned, it must be given. This may be the greatest lesson you will learn from this class. You have an open classroom, where you are given an unlimited number of options from which to choose. You must choose the extent to which you will pursue the game of tennis. You must choose your level of participation. You must choose how often you will attend class. You must choose the time you come to class and when you will leave. You must choose whether or not you will listen to my ideas. You must choose to accept them or not. And what is so important about your options in my class is the fact that with most of them, any negative impact on your grade will be negligible.

Because you have few restraints in my class, you will be free to choose, each day, a course of action which, according to your standard of life, is beneficial. What you must understand is that this freedom is beneficial only to the extent that you are willing to accept responsibility for your choices and actions. You can not enjoy freedom without accepting the responsibility of knowing that the limits of your right to pursue happiness begins with your power of volition and ends with the next person's right to do the same. You can not enjoy freedom without accepting the responsibility of knowing that every choice carries a consequence which, desired or not, must equally be embraced. And you can not enjoy freedom without accepting the responsibility of perspective, your capacity to view the vicissitudes of life from the broadest possible context.

What is true in my class is also true in life. You can not expect to reap the benefits of freedom without carrying the burden of responsibility. It is a packaged deal. And the extent to which you have learned how to accept responsibility is the extent to which you will make life choices that are beneficial to you and not harmful to anyone else.

Happiness, perspective, freedom, and responsibility are at the core of mental health. And the fullest expression of this quality of life is to be found in your capacity to seek, and exercise, options which are in *your rational best interest*, options which are for you and against no one. The challenge of mental health lies in the on-going process of looking for options, and is limited only by your desire. I recall a conversation I once had with two of my team members in a doubles match against the top seeded team in a tournament. They had lost the first set badly, and were losing the second when I decided to talk to them on a changeover. I could not help but notice that they were getting more discouraged with each lost game, so I wanted to help them, not with their physical skills, but with their perspective. First, I asked them if they had exercised every possible option as far as tactics were concerned, stating that if not, then they still had work to do because, as long as they had options, they had a chance to get back into the match. And as long as they had work to do, they did not have time to be discouraged. Second, I said that if they had exercised every possible option, and nothing worked, then all this meant was that the other team was "better." And if the other team was better, getting discouraged would not change the outcome anyway.

The quality of your life is, indeed, ultimately measured by your pursuit of options. And in a world where options are everywhere, and where we equally share the freedom and responsibility of volition, this challenge becomes even more critical to the state of mental health you experience. This is my view of mental health. And in the context of my role as a teacher, and my responsibility as a center of influence, helping you improve the quality of your life is more important to me than teaching you how to hit a better backhand.

This book, and the class for which it is written, has been created to address this challenge. I have stated from the beginning that teaching you how to hit a better backhand is not my top priority. Nor is it my mission to change your life. I will not teach you how to be happy; I will allow you to experience it. I will not broaden your perspective; I will give you information that you can use to see reality with more clarity. I will not teach you the meaning of freedom; I will allow you to experience it within the limits of my right, and the rights of your classmates, to do the same. I will not teach you responsibility; I will give it.

Finally, I have written this book to make a difference, one class, one lesson, and one student at a time. I have chosen this forum, my classroom, to allow you to sharpen the tools for success you already possess, and to recognize that your capacity to grow is limited only by your resources and imagination. ***Tennis For Everyone*** is just one more resource that you can use to better understand the game of tennis and the game of life.

Name:________________ Section:________________

Obstacles

Chapter Summary:________________________________

Action Step #1:________________________________

Action Step #2:________________________________

Name:________________ Section:____________________

Learning Efficacy

Chapter Summary:____

____

____

____

____

____

____

____

____

____

____

____

____

____

____

Action Step #1:____

____

Action Step #2:____

____

Name:__________________ Section:______________________

Emotions, Pressure and Stress

Chapter Summary:____

Action Step #1:____

Action Step #2:____

Name:________________ Section:____________________

Mental Health

Chapter Summary:____

Action Step #1:____

Action Step #2:____

Bibliography

Anthony, Dr. Robert. "The Ultimate Secrets of Total Self- Confidence." Berkeley Books, New York, NY 1984

Branden, Dr. Nathaniel. "The Art of Self-Discovery." Bantam Books, New York, NY 1993

_______. "Honoring the Self." Bantam Books, New York, NY 1985

_______. "How to Raise Your Self-Esteem." Bantam Books, New York, NY 1988

_______. "The Psychology of Self-Esteem." Bantam Books, New York, NY 1971

Frankl, Dr. Viktor E. "Man's Search for Meaning." Pocket Books, New York, NY 1984

Martens, Dr. Rainer. "Successful Coaching." Leisure Press, Champaign, IL 1990

Rand, Ayn. "For the New Intellectual." Random House, Inc., New York, NY 1961

_________. "Objectivism: The Philosophy of Ayn Rand." Penguin Books, New York, NY 1991

_________. "The Virtue of Selfishness." Penguin Books, New York, NY 1964